Friendship Quadrant

Copyright © 2017 by Friendship Quadrant

All rights reserved. This book or any portion thereof may not be reproduced or used in any manner whatsoever without the express written permission of the publisher except for the use of brief quotations in a book review.

Printed in the United States of America
First Printing, 2017
ISBN 978-0692935002

www.FriendshipQuadrant.com

Friendship

FQ

QUADRANT

BY: MICHAEL & KASSIE BOYD
WITH STEELE KIZERIAN

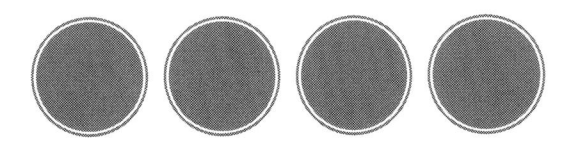

TESTIMONIALS

Having been in the counseling and corporate world for 21 years I have found that you can narrow the keys to happiness and success to a few critical principles. The Friendship Quadrant addresses several key proponents of individual success and fulfillment in relationships. I enjoyed reading this as a parent, a spouse, and as a business owner. The type of people you choose to surround yourself with has a deep impact on your trajectory in life. It has been one of the keys to my success. I work hard to surround myself with as many good people as possible. This book teaches us how to do that starting at a young age. Great read for teenagers and adults alike...

- J.D. Stacey, MSW

I can picture families all over the world benefiting from this simple, understandable book. I was literally underlining clues on almost every page. Your wise and powerful guidelines will help anyone choose good friends and learn how to be the friend everyone wants.

- Bryan Thayer, Trainer/ Author
Life Leaves Clues

We wish that we had this information as we were raising our five children. We have read a lot of parenting books and books about teenagers, but nothing gave us a concrete method for them to be able to evaluate their friendships. Now we are teaching this to our grandkids.

- Grandparents

I love this concept! I wish I had learned it when I was younger, but I'm very happy that my children are learning it now. I am enjoying watching them as they learn to apply these principles in their lives. I've seen them understand some difficult relationships with their friends and even make better choices in friends. You are never too young or too old for the Friendship Quadrant!

- Mother

The 'Friendship Quadrant' presentation was a life changing experience for many of my students. The seniors wished they had learned this information earlier. I now realize that most students group all friends in the same category, and by using the Quadrants it has helped them know what to expect from each of their friends. My students are still talking about the seminar and how they benefited from it.

This presentation should be heard by students of all ages to help them realize these differences. Since so many of our children are led by peer pressure, this method helps them recognize the value of their friends through these Quadrants. Once they understand these differences, they will be happier and more loyal individuals in school and in their future.

- High School Advisor

I know quadrant three friends can be fun, but they can also hurt my feelings. I want to find quadrant one friends…the true friends that I can just "click" with.

- Third Grade

Every high school senior ought to be required to take this short seminar on friendship before they continue on with their adult lives. In that tumultuous transition period, many people get mixed up with the wrong kind of friends and lose their own core values. Personally, this grounded my love for my best friends and reminded me of the kind of people I will be looking for when I attend a university in the fall!"

- High School Senior

The 'Friendship Quadrant' has helped me know if my friends are really good friends, or if they are just going to use me.

- High School Freshman

I liked to know about different kinds of friends. I didn't understand how important it is to look for "quadrant one" friends. I'm glad that I know more about friends, because I now can be a better friend. I think I'll stay away from quadrant four people. It is easy for me to evaluate my friends and put them in a category. This will help me forever!

- Eighth Grade

It has taught me who my true friends are, and who I can depend on. I have learned how to understand the friends that I am not sure about, and their loyalty. It has also helped me realize what I need to be like in order to be a true or best friend to others.

- High School Sophomore

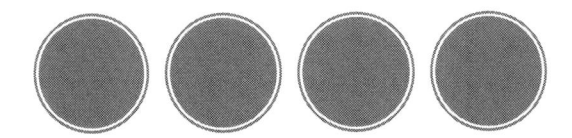

ACKNOWLEDGEMENTS

We realize that any endeavor like the Friendship Quadrant requires the insights and talents of others for the book to be truly worthwhile. Throughout this process, there have been many friends and relatives who have supported and encouraged our efforts. We are so grateful for all of their help. Truly, life's greatest treasures come in the form of these loving relationships.

However, there are four individuals that we want to recognize because their assistance has had such a direct and positive impact on this project. First, we want to recognize Jennifer Law. Jenny was invaluable to us with creative ideas and insights while we organized the layout of the book. She was so patient as we constantly made changes.

Secondly, Ciera Kizerian who provided her creative touch in designing the graphics for the book.

Next, we want to acknowledge our talented friend, Christy Wardle. We are amazed at all the things Christy excels at including her work as a graphic artist. Her bright and positive outlook on life benefited us greatly as she helped us put the finishing touches on the book and designed the cover.

And finally, Steele Kizerian, who has played a vital role in assisting us to finish and edit the book. Steele's insights, suggestions, additions, and hard work are reflected throughout the book as he helped to complete this project. Without Steele, the Friendship Quadrant would still be sitting on our computer.

INTRODUCTION

> "A FAITHFUL FRIEND IS BEYOND PRICE;
> NO SUM CAN BALANCE HIS WORTH."
>
> - SIRACH -

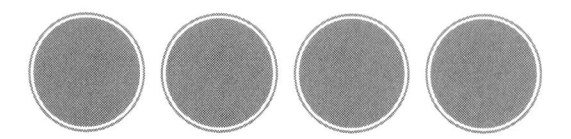

We've all experienced it. Someone you think is a "good" friend, or even a "best" friend, ends up disappointing you. When it happens, and it will happen, it can be one of the toughest moments in your life. It leaves you feeling empty and confused. It leaves you feeling betrayed and asking yourself, "What's wrong with me? What did I do wrong?"

We've all been there, and we've seen it happen to countless others, but when we saw it happen to our own child, the impact was much stronger--different somehow.

Our son, Sterling, had a friend down the street who acted like a "good friend" one day and then ignored him the next. He would make plans with Sterling and then if something better came along, he would ditch our son and run off with other friends, leaving Sterling feeling sad, lonely, and sometimes in tears.

Our inner "mama and papa bear" came out in us and we wanted to talk to this particular friend and his parents. We wanted to step in and fix the problem. It's pretty normal for concerned parents to desire to step in and "fix things" for their kids, but deep down, we knew that this wouldn't produce positive results. Perhaps in the short run--but definitely not in the long run. Let's be honest; it's hard enough to fix ourselves, much less anyone else. Besides, the more we do that, the less prepared our kids are for adulthood. What would that teach our son about dealing with the realities of life?

This dilemma pestered us for months. We read numerous parenting books, but to no avail. We couldn't find a solution to this problem. One afternoon we took a brisk walk in the mountains. We found ourselves discussing our kids and their friends. As we discussed the predicament, we had an epiphany. The light bulb went off and we realized that we needed to help our children choose their friends more wisely.

How much would that benefit them? A lot! We wondered if there was a way, perhaps a tool or a resource, which would help us teach our children this important skill. As we walked, the thoughts and ideas flowed and became the foundation for the Friendship Quadrant, a tool that empowers not only young people, but adults as well, in choosing friends wisely.

Perhaps just as important, it teaches us how to be a good friend. Learning the Friendship Quadrant will prove pivotal in your overall happiness.

Your friends, the people you associate with, have a direct impact on the course of your life. You don't need us to convince you of the truthfulness of that statement; just look at the examples that surround you.

It's our desire that the Friendship Quadrant will help you become the person you were destined to become. Having good friends is that powerful. We believe that, once you've read this book, you'll feel like Abraham Lincoln did when he said, "I'd like to believe that I'm smarter today than I was yesterday!"

Enjoy!

CHAPTER 1

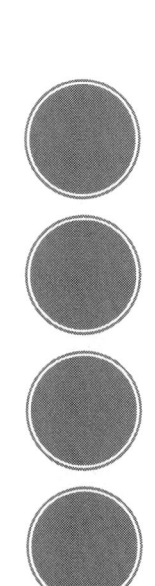

WHY YOU NEED
THE FRIENDSHIP QUADRANT

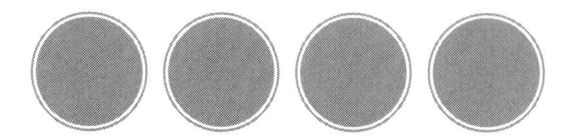

WHY YOU NEED THE FRIENDSHIP QUADRANT

Who you choose to continually associate with on a daily basis will impact who you become more than any other thing. This definitely applies to the friends you choose to be with today. These deliberate decisions, for they're decisions within your control, will mold and shape you and your future.

You make decisions from the moment you wake up in the morning until the time you go to bed. Most of them are pretty mundane decisions. What will I wear? What will I eat for breakfast? However, there are other critical decisions that will shape and mold your life forever. **The decision of whom your friends will be is one of those critical decisions and can't and shouldn't be treated lightly.**

That particular decision will have a lifelong impact that could mean the difference between happiness or sadness, success or failure.

To demonstrate the impact our friends have on the course of our lives, we share the story of Brandon. Brandon was dynamic, engaging, and smart. He was destined for great things. Our friends wanted that kind of example for their new son. So impressed were our friends with Brandon and his character that they actually named their son after him; however, one short year after their son was born, Brandon started hanging out with the wrong group of friends. These "friends" introduced Brandon to the vices of the world.

Soon, he became heavily involved in drugs and alcohol. While under the influence of alcohol, he had a serious car accident and almost died. The relatively quick change in Brandon's life was directly connected to his choice of friends. By hanging out with this new group of 'friends,' their negative influence was life-changing.

At every stage of life you have the opportunity to choose friends. This decision is made in elementary school, middle school, and high school. It's made in college, after college, at work, at church and/or other community organizations. These decisions are made over and over again.

This isn't a one-time thing. Within each phase of life, these decisions are made multiple times - we gain friends and we lose friends. The questions you have to ask yourself are: "How do I choose my friends? Is it a conscious decision? Do I look ahead and think about where this decision will take me?" Most of the friends you choose now won't be around in ten years, but their impact and influence may follow you forever.

> FINDING AND CULTIVATING GOOD FRIENDSHIPS IS IMPORTANT THROUGHOUT YOUR LIFE. YOUR FRIENDS ARE THE PEOPLE WITH WHOM YOU SPEND MOST OF YOUR TIME. THEY INFLUENCE YOUR CHOICES AS YOU ARE ESTABLISHING AND DISCOVERING YOUR OWN IDENTITY AND DEVELOPING PERSONAL HABITS.

Think back to the time when you were in elementary school. What was your thought process for choosing friends back then? Who were your friends? Why did you choose them? How did you choose them? What was your intent? What were you looking for? Most people will respond saying it wasn't a conscious decision. It was simply they enjoyed playing together. What you were looking for then is much different than what you are looking for now. What are you looking for now? What's your criteria now for choosing friends? Are your friends from Kindergarten still your friends today?

Why or why not? What made you change? What made them change? As you get older and enter middle school, high school, college, etc. there seems to be a pivotal period for many where the moment of truth arrives and new friends are chosen and old friends are left behind, sometimes for the better, and other times for worse.

Sarah grew up in California and went to the same elementary school from K-6th grade. She developed many strong friendships. She and her friends hung out every single day after school. They were so excited to finally "graduate" from elementary school and attend middle school. They talked about their plans for the summer and classes they wanted to take next year. They were excited to meet new boys and girls from the other schools in the area. Middle school finally arrived and Sarah was so excited! She saw her group of friends and ran up to them all giddy. They all talked about their assigned classes. A few months passed, but something strange happened. Sarah noticed that her group didn't hang out together after school, like they used to in elementary school. Many of her close friends started to hang out with older, more popular kids. They slowly ignored her. Before she knew it, her strong friendships from elementary school were no more. Some even laughed at her and made fun of her as she would pass them in the halls. Some got serious with boys. Others started smoking and drinking. Sarah couldn't believe it. What happened? What changed? What did she do wrong?

Sarah didn't do anything wrong. Her friends made choices to choose new friends, even if those choices were for the worse. It was their pivotal moment, but unfortunately, it wasn't for the better.

Regarding choice, author Jim Rohn, said, "Every life form seems to strive to its maximum except human beings. How tall will a tree grow? As tall as it possibly can. Human beings, on the other hand, have been given the ability to choose. You can choose to be more, or you can choose to be less. Why not stretch up to the full measure of the challenge and see how much you can do and be?"

Why do you need the Friendship Quadrant? A well-known speaker visited with teenagers around the world. She asked all of them the same questions and the answers were almost always the same:

>What makes you happy? Friends.

>What are your greatest worries? Friends.

>What do you like to do in your free time? Be with friends.

>Why do you go to church? To be with friends.

>What helps you make good choices? Good friends.

>When do you feel the most pressure to do something bad? With my friends.

Clearly, friends are a vital part of your life. They can be the greatest ... or the worst influence in your life.

We frequently talk to young people about their future. They

have some great dreams, yet those dreams can be easily lost because of the negative influence of the wrong friends. Sure, it's not always this extreme, but because they choose the wrong friends, millions of teens question the very thing that's so valuable to their success in life–their self-worth. They question what they know to be true.

Healthy relationships with friends can be a great source of self-worth. We need good friends, and we want to feel accepted. We desire confidence and want to feel important. One of the greatest motivators in life is the desire to be validated, or appreciated, for who you are. You might appear to be one of the most successful or popular kids in school, but inside, you may be hurting because you haven't found the type of positive friends who appreciate you for who you really are and help build you up. In short, you have to change who you are to be their friend.

Again, the Friendship Quadrant is a personal and private tool that will help you make vital decisions regarding friends. When you comprehend the Friendship Quadrant, you'll understand how to recognize a true friend, and more importantly, how to be a true friend. You'll learn that you always have a choice. You're in control of the friends you choose. This isn't a tool for judging others harshly. Rather, it's a <u>reliable compass to guide you in the friendship process.</u>

25

In the eyes of those around her, Terri had everything. She was "popular" in all of the ways a teen wants to be popular. She was beautiful, active in school leadership, strongly committed to living her values, and was even voted homecoming queen; yet, despite her apparent achievements, she wasn't happy.

She felt responsible for making her friends happy, but didn't know how. She felt she was always giving and they were always taking. They complained about school, their parents, their lives, and even about each other. Often, they would make plans without her, leaving her feeling like an outsider, and wondering, "What's wrong with me?" Eventually she realized that she couldn't count on her 'friends.' They were playing a highly dramatic game, and it wasn't much fun for anyone.

Terry believed there was something wrong with her. Once she learned about the Friendship Quadrant, her entire outlook changed. She stopped second-guessing herself, thinking that if she could just make her friends happy, she would feel happy, too. She felt empowered! She learned that the type of friends she chose to associate with really did matter.

As an example, when our daughter Savannah was in fifth grade, she was riding home from school in our neighbor's car. Our neighbor's child was crying because of something one of her friends had said to her at school. Savannah quickly (and unemotionally) said, "Sounds like a Quadrant 3 to me!" She then went on to explain to her friend all about the Friendship Quadrant and how to use it on her own. At age ten, she was able to use the Friendship Quadrant as a tool to help her neighbor through a tough situation. Savannah didn't judge, ridicule nor gossip about the situation; she simply observed that the problem lay with the other little girl, not with her friend.

As you learn how the Friendship Quadrant works, don't be too hard on yourself for any past mistakes you may have made regarding your choice of friends. Our past should be like a school that we learn from, not a stick with which we continually beat ourselves up.

You may recognize that you don't feel as good about yourself because of your choice of friends. When you begin to realize that it could possibly be them and not you, you'll feel empowered, and some important things will start to make sense, finally.

Good friends can make life so much easier; poor friends can drag you down into unhappiness and, potentially, into trouble. True friends can be your greatest source of strength, while unreliable friends can create doubt and despair. It doesn't matter how tough you think you are. We all need good, reliable friends whom we can count on.

The teenage years have been described as a time of *Identity Theft!* Teenagers must arm themselves with tools to help them navigate through life. It can be a time of great confusion. So often, teenagers allow others to define who they are. *Stop it!* Don't let the actions of other people confuse you and rob you of your true identity!

What if you could easily learn how to discern who is truly a "good friend" and who isn't? Knowledge like that would even help you become a better friend, and in turn, it can actually help your current friends learn how to be better friends ... if they choose to be. Let's focus on you first. Why would you choose to hang out with anyone who is a negative influence on you? Why would you choose to hang out with anyone that makes you feel less about yourself or harms your self-image? We all have done it at some point. Why? What good came out of it? Why do we put ourselves through the misery? This is the friend who will often encourage you to do things you know are wrong.

Many times, this is the friend who at a moment's notice will 'dis' you to go to a better party or hang out with "cooler" people. These types of people are all around you. You have to learn to recognize and identify what quadrant a person/friend is in so that you can manage your expectations and mitigate your risk of getting hurt.

> "AVOID NEGATIVE PEOPLE AT ALL COSTS.
> THEY ARE THE GREATEST DESTROYERS
> OF SELF-CONFIDENCE AND SELF-ESTEEM.
> SURROUND YOURSELF WITH PEOPLE WHO
> BRING OUT THE BEST IN YOU."
> – BRIAN TRACY

One of the main goals of the Friendship Quadrant is to help stimulate conversation between parents and children, teachers and students, teens and their peers. We hope we're able to help you or someone you care about to increase both your sense of self-worth and self-awareness. It's our desire that the Friendship Quadrant will help you become the person you were destined to become.

We know that once you've read the Friendship Quadrant, you'll understand that great friendships based on trust can, and will, have a direct impact on your personal happiness. More important, you'll know how to create, foster and keep these amazing friendships.

"I URGE YOU TO CHOOSE AND CHERISH
THOSE FRIENDS WHO LIFT YOU AND MAKE
YOU BETTER IN THEIR PRESENCE.
AND BE SUCH FRIENDS TO ONE ANOTHER."

–RUSSELL M. NELSON

"A good friend is honest and sincere, someone who will reach out to me and to others. They look me in the eye and greet me by name. They listen when I share my feelings and are willing to trust me and share in return. Our conversations aren't one-sided. They kindly remind me when I'm doing something that isn't right. They encourage and support me in my beliefs even if our values aren't the same. They think of my feelings before they do something. They're willing to apologize. Good friends help you to be more forgiving and open to say 'I'm sorry.' I know that I'm a better person because of the friends I keep around me—they help me to keep my standards, without tempting me to do something they know I don't want to do."

- Jennifer, 17 years old

CHAPTER 2

THE
FRIENDSHIP QUADRANT MODEL

COMPATABILITY → FQ

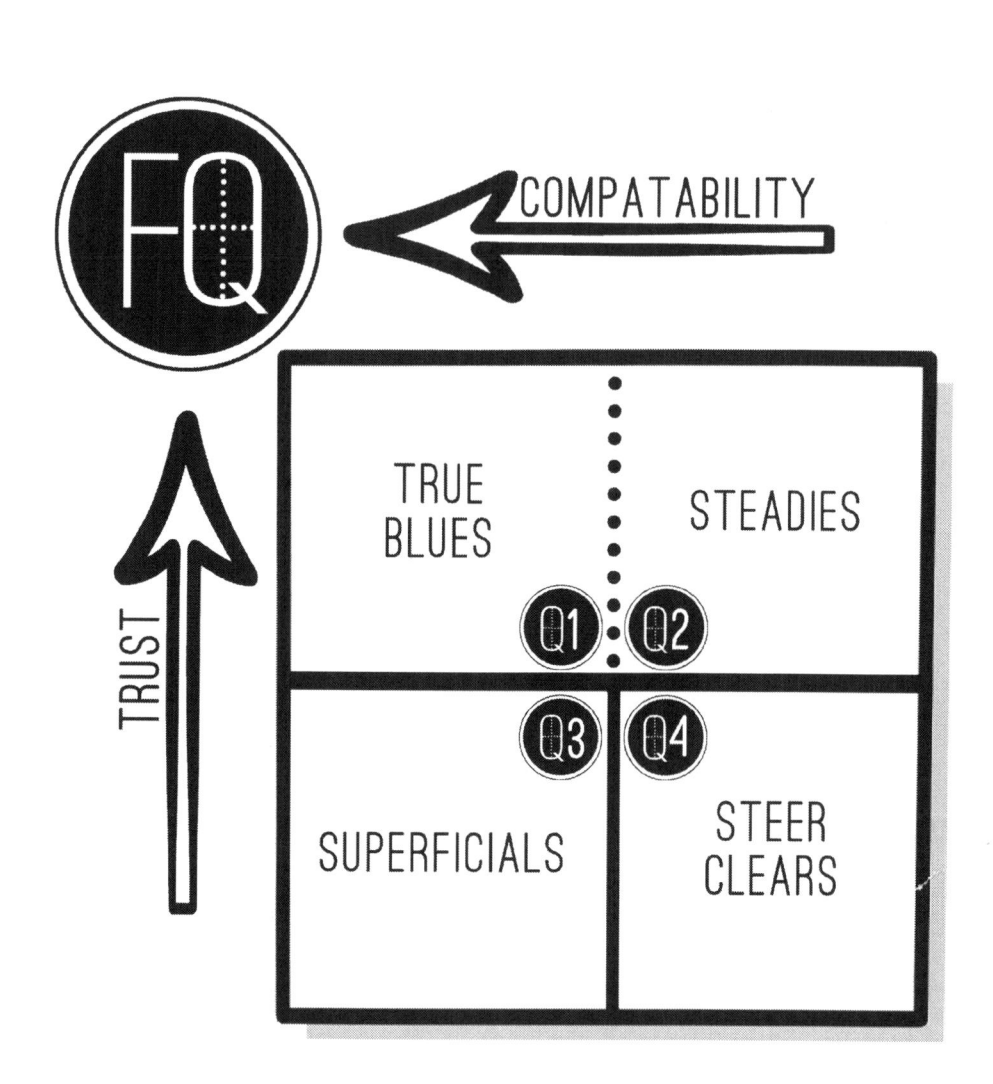

TRUST ↑

TRUE BLUES	STEADIES
Q1 Q2	
Q3 Q4	
SUPERFICIALS	STEER CLEARS

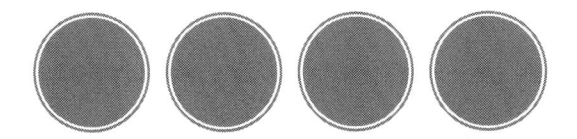

THE FRIENDSHIP QUADRANT MODEL

The Friendship Quadrant will primarily focus on the people you know. These are the people you have had enough interaction with to make an initial assessment of who they are. In the following chapters, you'll learn that most people fall into one of four quadrants, hence the Friendship Quadrant. Each quadrant has its own set of characteristics that define a type of friend. Keep in mind, we all at one time or another have moments where we might fall into different categories. This is not set in stone, but it is a good barometer and tool.

FRIENDSHIP QUADRANT MODEL

Quadrant 1 - TRUE BLUES:
They have all the qualities of a true friend.

Quadrant 2 - STEADIES:
They are great people who are also good friends.

Quadrant 3 - SUPERFICIALS:
They are fun yet unreliable friends.

Quadrant 4 - STEER CLEARS:
The people you should avoid.

UNKNOWNS

Unknowns are the people you haven't had enough encounters with to know which quadrant they initially will be in. Many of them have 'untapped potential,' meaning many of them potentially can become good and maybe even great friends. Imagine a big pool. All of your 'knowns' are already in the pool. These are the people inside the Friendship Quadrant. The rest of the world is outside the pool. All of your friendships, at one point or another, start "outside the pool." For those inside the pool, you already know which "quadrant" of the pool they're in. Unknowns aren't yet classified as friends; rather, they're more of an acquaintance.

These are the neighbors, classmates, and strangers you've yet to meet, or with whom you've had minimal interaction.

In a sense, they haven't jumped into the pool yet. You simply don't associate with them enough to make an assessment of what type of friend they may become. You don't have enough experiences with them to know if you're compatible or if you can trust them. If they do jump into the pool, you don't know which "quadrant" of the pool they'll be in yet. They have the potential to become True Blues (Q1) and/or Steadies (Q2).

My neighbor was an unknown until the night my family moved. We'd been living in our home for five years. We had to be out of our home in a hurry. It was just after Thanksgiving. The day was rainy, windy, and cold. Some neighbors and friends came for a period of time. Others apologized because of bad timing, but Mike Chapman, my neighbor who was always friendly but quiet and unassuming, showed up and never left my side. Even when it was late and our clothes were freezing wet he was there until the final items were placed or shoved into the additional rental storage unit.

I can still remember my emotions as the large metal door finally came down. It was over. I was exhausted. Mike smiled, put his hand out, and said, "Is there anything else you need help with tonight?" That night I realized that I had missed out on, what could have been, a really good friendship!

They also have the potential to be Superficials (Q3) and even Steer Clears (Q4). The FQ Model helps you to recognize flags, warnings, concerns, as well as positive clues of the type of friend a person is or may become.

The two axes (yes this is plural for "axis") of the Friendship Quadrant are Trust and Compatibility. These are the foundational principles of the Friendship Quadrant.

Friendships are created, fostered, and grown based on these principles; they're also ruined, destroyed, and lost with the lack of these principles.

TRUST

Every positive, lasting, and meaningful friendship has a high degree of trust. What is trust? According to Merriam-Webster's dictionary, trust is defined as **"a firm belief in the integrity, ability, effectiveness, or genuineness of someone or something."** If a relationship has trust, it also has the following qualities: honesty, reliability, honor, and respect. This is the standard by which you should measure the quality of your friendships. Ask yourself if your friends are trustworthy. More important, are **you** trustworthy? Do **you** exemplify these characteristics of trust?

As you fully know, trust must be earned. Once lost, it's difficult to get back. Do everything in your power to surround yourself with people you can trust.

True Blues and Steadies are above the horizontal line which represent the line of trust. You should always strive to personally be

"Above the Line of Trust" and to find friends who are as well. If your friends are "Below the Line of Trust", you can be left alone, hurt, confused, and sometimes even in danger. If you're "Below the Line of Trust," **Step Up and Stay Up!** Constantly think "Stay Above the Line of Trust" (SALT). Let that be your motto.

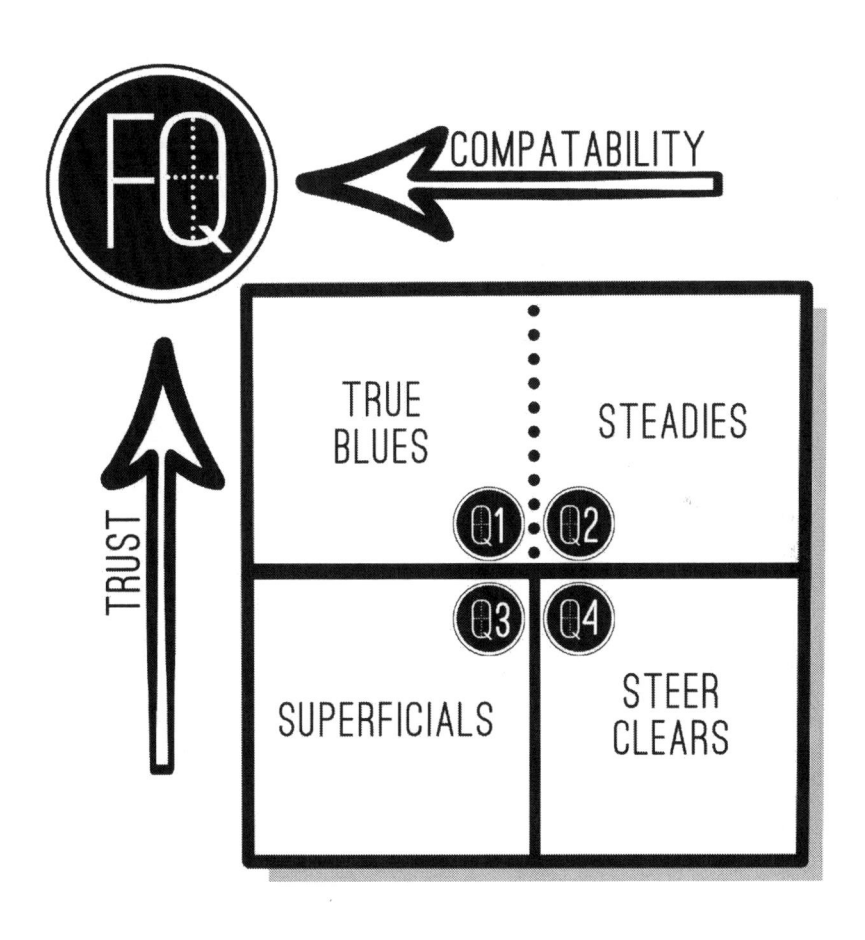

FQ ← COMPATABILITY

↑ TRUST

	TRUE BLUES	STEADIES
	Q1	Q2
	Q3	Q4
	SUPERFICIALS	STEER CLEARS

COMPATIBILITY

Compatibility is a vital part of our friendships. It's the fun part, the part of friendships where we find the most joy. The more compatible the friendship, the richer the relationship. There are many good friendships out there that are high on trust, but low on compatibility. We'll get into this later, but the deepest friendships around are those that are high in trust and high in compatibility. When we say compatibility, what we're really saying is getting along, having fun, sharing common interests/desires/dreams/hobbies, etc. It's something that can't be forced. It's a natural and important facet of any lasting relationship.

STAY ABOVE THE LINE OF

TRUST

CHAPTER 3

THE INTENT OF THE
FRIENDSHIP QUADRANT MODEL

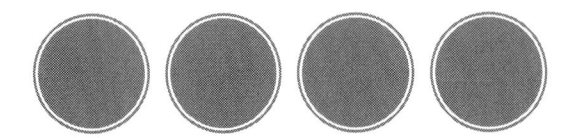

THE INTENT OF THE FRIENDSHIP QUADRANT MODEL

PERMANENTLY LABELING

The Friendship Quadrant isn't about permanently labeling others into a certain quadrant. It's not "once a superficial, always a superficial." You have to allow people a chance to make mistakes, to change, and to improve. There's no such thing as a perfect friend.

There will be times when your truest friend will disappoint you. Don't be quick to "downgrade" that friend to a Superficial (Q3) because of one small instance. You don't always know the full story. You don't know what circumstances people are going through. Be patient, understanding, and forgiving.

Rebecca and Carla not only have been sisters-in-law, but have been close and dear friends for over twenty years. They have been there for each other through all the good times and the bad. These two are True Blue (Q1) friends. One day, Rebecca and Carla were with some other friends and family members. Rebecca went off with the other friends to grab a dessert and didn't invite Carla. Carla's feelings were hurt. Rebecca's intent wasn't to hurt her feelings. Instead of letting it fester and ruin the friendship, the two of them discussed their feelings. Rebecca quickly apologized and Carla quickly forgave. Although Rebecca had her Superficial (Q3) moment, it wasn't the overall pattern in her typical behavior, so Carla didn't let it impact the friendship and the two remain great True Blue (Q1) friends

You'll want the same treatment when you disappoint your closest friends. People make mistakes. It boils down to motive and intent.

Was that friend really trying to disappoint you?
Does this happen on a consistent basis?
What's the overall pattern of the friendship?

Just because you think someone may be saying something hurtful doesn't make it so. Just because you see a situation and think it's one way doesn't make it so. You and your friends will have moments when you act like superficials, but for the most part they're temporary.

Think of it this way--you can have years, of a True Blue (Q1) or Steady (Q2) friendship; would you throw that away because of one Superficial (Q3) moment? Will that exception to the norm determine the rest of the friendship in the future? The answer to that is up to you. It may depend on what that moment was.

Life is hard. On any given day, a friend can be the absolute best or the absolute worst. Every day there's a circumstance that can change a person for a few hours or a few days or even forever. Perhaps those actions would have been different if the circumstance had been different. Sometimes you will be a steady friend, a true blue friend, or even a superficial friend. You can't be everything to everyone all of the time.

Don't expect perfection out of your friends--you won't get it. Again, look at the overall pattern of the friendship to help guide you in the hard moments of your friendships.

Well, it's time for a confession. When I was in middle school, I auditioned for, and got the part of Dorothy in the "Wizard of Oz." I guess I thought it was kind of cool. I was in the bathroom with a friend, and I said to her, "Can you believe that Laura tried out for Dorothy, too?" We both laughed.

Then, guess who came walking out of the stall? Yep. Laura. She came right up to me and said, "Thanks a lot, Kassie. I thought we were friends." I've never felt so low nor so sad.

I vowed then and there that I would never speak unkindly about another person again. That "yucky" feeling has stayed with me, and even today when I think about that incident, I feel sad. I was definitely a Superficial (Q3) that day to Laura, but I committed myself to be a better friend from that day forward! So remember--people can change!

MANAGE EXPECTATIONS

This tool will help you identify where you, and each of your friends, currently are in the Friendship Quadrant. By doing so, you'll be able to recognize patterns and tendencies that will help you manage expectations.

PROTECT

The Friendship Quadrant is also meant to protect you. Today, there are millions of adults who wish they had made better decisions in the friend department when they were younger. If you can recognize early on that a certain group of people won't be good for your future, you'll save yourself from a lot of pain and regret.

BECOME

Change requires effort, patience, discipline, and desire. As you apply the principles in this book, you will learn how to become a better friend. In addition, your energy will be put into relationships that uplift you, therein fostering an environment to become your best self.

Our friend shared the following with us:

"Years ago when I was in middle school, a new girl moved to the area. One night, all of my girlfriends and I were hanging out. As the night evolved, our conversation kept going back to making fun of the new girl. We were gossiping and speaking poorly of her. The next Monday, the new girl confronted me. I felt ashamed and disappointed. I can picture this moment so vividly because I knew better. She even said to me, "I didn't think you would be a part of it."

"Actually, I didn't even say anything bad about her, but I didn't say anything to stop what was happening either. I apologized and thankfully she forgave me. We maintained a friendship throughout middle school. I'll never forget that moment. Since then, I've tried to always defend those who aren't present."

CHAPTER 4

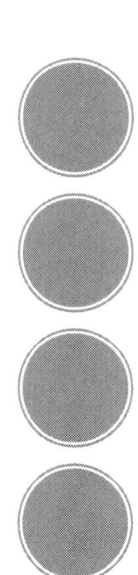

Q4

STEER
CLEARS

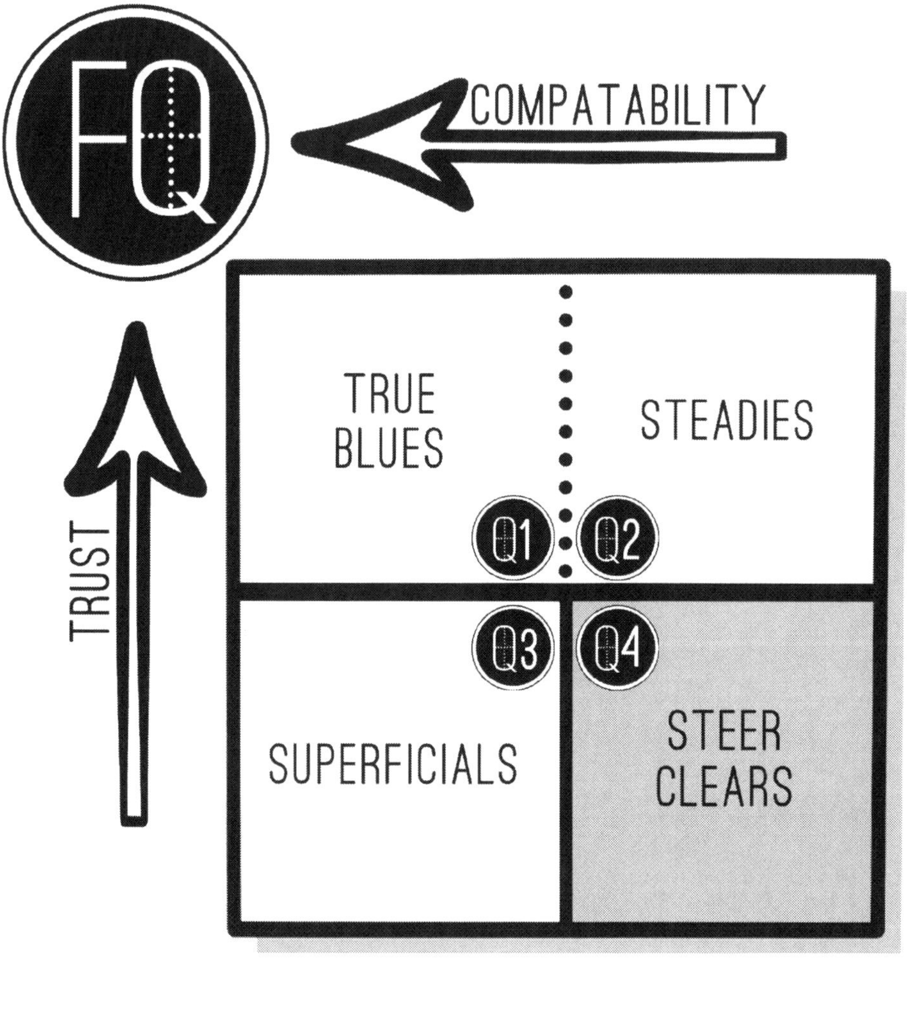
FQ
COMPATABILITY
TRUST
TRUE BLUES
STEADIES
Q1
Q2
Q3
Q4
SUPERFICIALS
STEER CLEARS

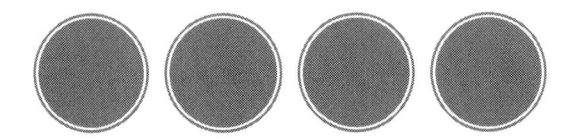

QUADRANT 4: THE STEER CLEARS

A Q4, The Steer Clear, dwells in the Low Trust, Low Compatibility quadrant. This quadrant contains the people you don't want to be associating with--at all. You don't have anything in common and you don't trust them. In this group, they're generally the type of people you know to stay away from if you can. You don't share similar values nor behaviors. If you didn't have a specific connection, (classmate, neighbor, teammate or even relative) you wouldn't choose to associate with this person.

Steer Clears can be bullies, gossips, jerks, disturbers, and destroyers. They're usually jealous, selfish, rude, mean, and inconsiderate. Often they're the type of person who will do anything to get ahead in life. They can be downright hurtful and

FQ

We don't always get to choose whom we work with. This was the case with one of our friends.

Sam worked at a local restaurant. Many of the guys he had to work with weren't the type of people with whom he would choose to spend time. They were crude; they swore, smoked, and frequented bars late into the night. He was frustrated with his work environment; however, he realized he had to find a way to interact with them without compromising his standards. Tricky to do!

Eventually, he had to find another job because he knew the influences around him were negative and detrimental.

Clearly, Sam's co-workers were Steer Clears (Q4)

dangerous to your self-esteem. They'll usually make you doubt your own self-worth. They'll make you feel that you're the problem. They'll belittle you, demean you, manipulate you, and make fun of you.

Do your best not to be alone with them.

A STEER CLEAR (Q4) IS SELFISH

Steer Clears can be like crabs. A single crab in a lidless bucket is bound to escape, yet when more than one crab shares a bucket, none of them can get out. If one crab elevates itself above the rest, the other crabs will grab it and drag it back down to share the common fate of the other crabs. So it is with Q4's. Some find themselves associating with people who continually pull them down while they strive to better themselves.

Don't let "crabs" discourage you. Find those you can trust, those who "Stay Above the Line of Trust," who will pull you up and out of that bucket!

A STEER CLEAR (Q4) OFTEN GOSSIPS

Steer Clears are quick to engage in gossip. They thrive on the opportunity to tear people down and make them as miserable as possible. Typically, Steer Clears are unhappy themselves and want others to be the same.

We're reminded of the story of an old man who was the unfair victim of gossip. When the young gossiper apologized and offered to make it better, the old man simply asked him to take a large pillow up to the top of the highest building on the day when the wind blew hardest. Once there, the young man was to cut open the pillow and let all the feathers be carried away by the wind. That was easy enough.

After fulfilling his assignment the young man reported back to the older man. "Good," replied the old man, "now go and collect all the feathers you released." The young man couldn't do it. Once gossip is spread, it can't be completely collected again. **Gossip can never be entirely undone.**

A STEER CLEAR (Q4) AFFECTS SELF-ESTEEM

We have a tendency to correlate the behavior of others to our own self-worth. When someone does something unkind to you, it's natural to wonder, What's wrong with me? or Why aren't they being nice to me?

If you aren't feeling good about your relationships with other people, it can have a negative impact on your self-worth. By staying near people who treat you poorly, you're telling them it's okay to do so. Steer Clears will always end up treating you poorly. They'll always make you doubt your own self-worth. They'll make you feel that you're the problem.

> GREAT PEOPLE TALK ABOUT IDEAS.
> AVERAGE PEOPLE TALK ABOUT THINGS.
> SMALL PEOPLE TALK ABOUT OTHER PEOPLE.

As we stated earlier, Steer Clears will belittle you, demean you, manipulate you, and make fun of you.

If you discover that you're spending too much time around those "Below the Line of Trust"--The Superficials (Q3) and the Steer Clears (Q4)--take a step back and evaluate your friendships. Commit to quickly moving on to making new and stronger friendships.

HAVE COURAGE

Once you recognize a person is a Steer Clear (Q4), have the courage to distance yourself from them, as soon as possible. It's in your best interest. They don't do any good for you. A Steer Clear (Q4) is going nowhere fast.

An example of a young man steering clear is Jacob.

Jacob enjoyed track in high school. He enjoyed the physical exercise, the challenge, and the camaraderie on the track; however, when not training, the rest of his teammates had different interests. He was continually invited to hang out or party with them on weekends. He knew that those parties weren't in his best interest and directly opposed his values. He wasn't comfortable with their interests or their choices, so he politely declined when they invited him to participate. He didn't trust them nor did he have much in common with them.

They associated on the field because they were a team, but he didn't feel the need nor the obligation to associate off the track, and that's okay!"

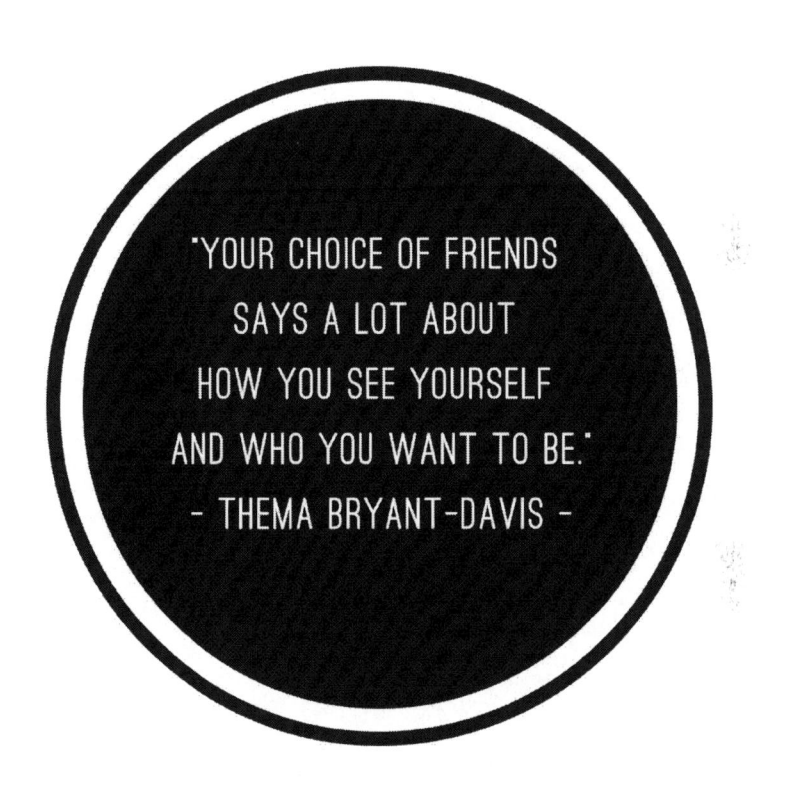

"YOUR CHOICE OF FRIENDS
SAYS A LOT ABOUT
HOW YOU SEE YOURSELF
AND WHO YOU WANT TO BE."
- THEMA BRYANT-DAVIS -

We moved to a new city when our daughter was in seventh grade. On her first day of school, she walked into the cafeteria and approached a group of girls.

She said, "Hello, I'm new, can I sit with you?" All of the girls laughed, rolled their eyes and turned the other way. Seriously?! We thought this only happened in silly, over-exaggerated movies.

When she came home, she told us about her day by saying, "Well, I met some Steer Clears today!"

We were so glad she had this tool to use, not that it made the situation less painful, but it did make it more understandable. Her ability to recognize them as Steer Clears allowed her to not beat herself up and to move forward looking for different/better friends.

CHAPTER 5

Q3

THE SUPERFICIALS

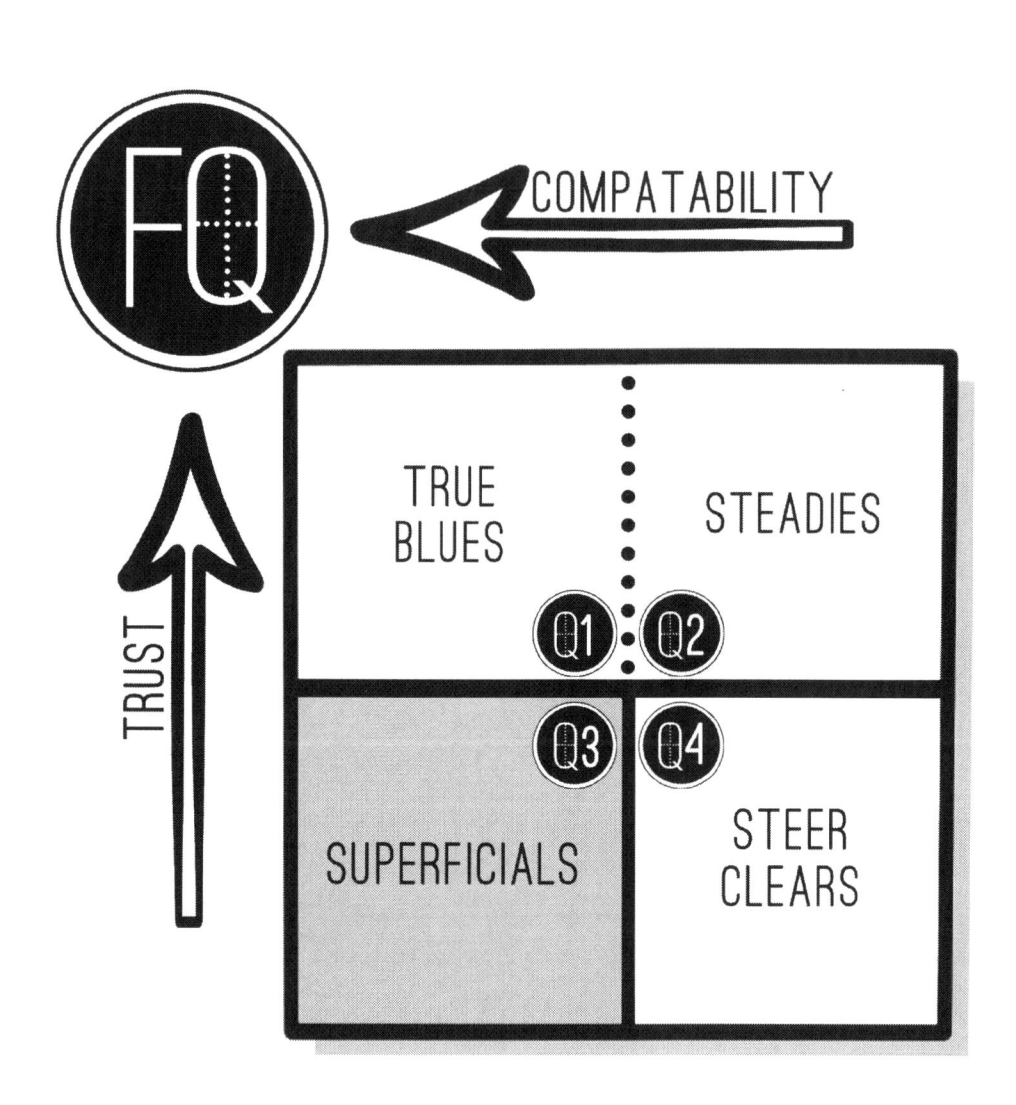

FQ

COMPATABILITY

TRUST

TRUE BLUES

STEADIES

Q1 Q2

Q3 Q4

SUPERFICIALS

STEER CLEARS

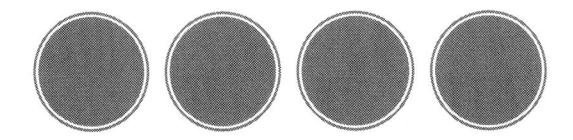

QUADRANT 3: THE SUPERFICIALS

A Superficial (Q3) dwells in the High Compatibility, Low Trust Quadrant. These friends can be fun, and friendly when they choose to be. These friends can be hot one day, and cold the next. You can't rely on them to be loyal to you. You can't trust them with your innermost worries, concerns, troubles, hardships, secrets, etc. because you don't know if they'll keep it to themselves or use it against you in the future. In some areas, they may be trustworthy, but in others they're not.

This is what makes them challenging: you don't know when you can trust them. Superficials aren't necessarily bad people whom you should avoid. Many times they're good friends. However, you can't fully rely on them to "have your back". In this chapter, we'll go over some of the warning signs and clues to help you recognize and identify friends who may fall into this quadrant. You may find that you yourself are in this quadrant.

A SUPERFICIAL CAN BE A USER

Superficials want to be around you as long as they can benefit from you in some way. They like you for what you have, whether it's a car, the latest video game, a cute brother, your money, your intellect, etc. When what you have can help them, they're there for you; however, when they don't need you anymore, you can't count on them.

A SUPERFICIAL CAN BE FLAKY

The bottom line is that Superficials will commit to hang out with you, but if a better offer comes along they'll 'dis' you. If you know and understand this type of 'friend,' you won't be disappointed when he lets you down. This is perhaps the greatest way the Friendship Quadrant is a tool and a resource. It will help you manage your expectations. We aren't saying to ditch all of your Superficial friends. We aren't preaching exclusion; rather, the opposite. You can still spend time with Superficials, just don't be disappointed when they change plans in the last minute or they don't measure up to what a True Blue/Steady friend is like.

Superficials can be like a chameleon, sometimes hidden and always changing. They're a friend of *convenience*, but usually *their* convenience. They can be warm and charming at times, but then they can also be rude and thoughtless. Their behavior can make you feel confused and cause you to doubt yourself. You may begin to think there's something wrong with you - when the problem is really *them*. They can cause deep scars on your heart and big dents in your confidence.

Mitch was Student Body President, team captain, Prom royalty, and one of the most popular kids at school. He knew everybody and everybody knew him. The majority of his friends were the popular crowd--the football players, cheerleaders, athletes, etc.

Here is his story: "Prom was coming up and my friends asked if the after-party could be at my home where there wouldn't be alcohol. A few days before the dance (and after all the food had already been purchased) my friends told me they were going to another party first, where there was alcohol, then they would go to my home after. I couldn't believe it and was shocked. I couldn't believe how flaky and disloyal my friends were being. Turned out, to my dismay and disappointment, that instead of sixty people showing up, there were only two. Eventually more showed up, but it wasn't until after they went to their first party of choice. Everyone treated me the same at school on Monday, but I felt different about the people who had responded with a "yes" but then went to the other party. They all made excuses about why they weren't there or were late. It was at that moment that I realized I had surrounded myself with the wrong friends."

Jessica explains how things were with her friend in high school:

"Julie is one of the most entertaining and fun people I know. She's witty and talented, so being around her is infectious. In the rare chance you get her one-on-one, she's a great listener and advice giver. However, 85% of the time we plan to hang out, she bails.

"I know she wasn't doing it intentionally, but it got old fast, so I stopped putting forth the effort."

> "WITH Q3'S YOU GET THE FEELING THEY MAKE PLANS WITH YOU BECAUSE THEY'VE GOT NOTHING BETTER TO DO AND YOU WERE THE LAST PERSON ON THEIR CALL LIST."
> -SARAH, AGE 14

It's easy to become confused when you spend too much time with a Superficial. You find yourself trying so hard to fit in and be part of the group. Your character, self-worth, and personality can all be tested. You begin to doubt your own motivation for doing something. Your confusion may lead you to try to please your Superficial friends. You might do foolish things with them that you will later regret.

A SUPERFICIAL OFTEN GOSSIPS

Often, you notice how they talk negatively about other "close friends" when those friends aren't around. This usually indicates that they talk badly about you when you are not present.

> "YOU CAN JUDGE THE CHARACTER OF OTHERS BY HOW THEY TREAT THOSE WHO CAN DO NOTHING TO THEM OR FOR THEM."
> -MALCOLM FORBES-

James Dobson, Christian psychologist, said that many adults still carry around the scars they got while in middle school.

For example, a seventh grader, Lori, told us about a girl in her class, Bethany, who was nice to her when no one else was around, but ignored her when others were present. One day, while Lori was talking with another friend, Bethany approached the two girls chatting. She rudely interrupted their conversation by standing right between the two girls, turned her back to Lori, blatantly ignoring her, and invited the other girl to go to a movie.

Lori was hurt, confused, and sad. She thought that maybe she did something wrong to merit such rude behavior, but couldn't pinpoint any such occasion. What Lori needs to realize is that nothing is wrong with her. The problem is Bethany.

At this moment in Bethany's life, she chose to be a Superficial (Q3).

A person who gossips about others behind their back is someone you simply can't trust. Be careful with others' reputations. Information you know about others should be kept in your "vault," in other words, they should feel "safe" with you and know that you won't share information.

Remember, Superficials are tricky because they can be fun, exciting, enjoyable and entertaining; however they can quickly turn on you by being unreliable, fickle and sometimes even back-stabbing. They can often be cruel and intimidating in their teasing, but then turn around and claim they were "just kidding." If you have to say "just kidding", then you most likely shouldn't say it at all. Be careful if this is the type of friend with whom you like to associate. Recognize who your superficial friends are so that you're prepared when they let you down.

A SUPERFICIAL CAN BE A NEGATIVE INFLUENCE

Another characteristic of a Superficial is when he appears to be loyal in every way, yet doesn't truly have your best interest at heart. The intent may be good, but the reality is that he doesn't consider how his poor choices and behavior can or will negatively impact your life. This is the friend who entices you to "try new things" and "live a little" by participating in behaviors that will negatively impact your life.

These choices or behaviors may include drugs, pornography, drinking, theft, vandalism, pre-marital sex, gambling, lying, cheating, and any other behavior that may provide a temporary "thrill." These behaviors or choices could lead you in a direction that will bring sadness and disappointment into your life and may even cause you physical harm.

So many kids are swayed by peer pressure to do things they wouldn't normally do on their own, and they do these things with kids who won't stand by them in the end.

Don't make a decision with a "friend" that will negatively affect the rest of your life. Don't risk an incredible future simply to belong to a crowd that won't care what happens to you later on down the road.

A Superficial clearly can be a negative influence. Be careful about going someplace alone with one or more Superficials. You could find yourself stuck/abandoned/coerced to do something you'll later regret.

A SUPERFICIAL CAN BE DECEPTIVE

Though Superficials appear to be good friends on the surface, they can be like the Trojan Horse; their outward appearance contradicts who they truly are on the inside.

The legend of the Trojan Horse comes from ancient Greek history depicting the ten-year war between the Greeks and the Trojans. Appearing to "give up" after a decade of laying siege on Troy, the Greeks left behind a gift to the goddess Athena as an offering for her protection on their long journey home. They then boarded their ships and sailed for home.

The Trojans were led to believe that the horse had been built so largely as to prevent them from bringing it inside their city, and thus claiming the blessing of Athena for themselves. The Trojans fell for the deception and pridefully pulled the horse inside their city gates, celebrating their apparent victory.

When Rex was about seven years old, he had a friend he liked very much. They walked home from school together.

One day, they stood by the road arguing about who was the faster runner. When Rex insisted that he was, his friend said to him, "If you're so fast, I dare you to run across the road before that car gets here!"

Rex saw a car a short distance away. He dashed into the road to prove he was fast and brave. A moment later the car's brakes squealed! The bumper hit Rex and he landed in an unconscious heap. When he opened his eyes, he saw his mother's worried face. His body was aching, his pride was hurt, and he realized that he hadn't been fast nor brave-- only foolish!

Meanwhile, during the night, a brave group of Greek men quietly left their hiding places in the bowels of the wooden horse and opened the city's gate for the Greek army which had returned in their ships under the cover of night. The Greeks finally conquered Troy after so many years of failure. **All thanks to their deception!**

Appearing to be better friends than they actually are, Superficials' inconsistent nature can be dangerous in two distinct ways.

1) They truly want to be your friend and thus have many of the traits of a True Blue in Q1 and a Steady in Q2, but because they're weak in choosing good behavior they often try to entice you to join them in their poor decisions.

2) One day they make you feel like you're their best friend, and the next day make you feel like a total stranger. They may unfairly criticize you or ignore you for the company of other "friends." The worst part of this is how it can make you question your own personal worth, wondering if you're the problem.

We spoke with Jared, a man in his forties, who was still haunted by something he was involved in as a teenager. He was out one night with several Superficials. He wasn't doing anything bad, but as the night went on, the group of guys started doing destructive and mean spirited petty vandalism to Michelle's home (a girl they knew). He felt "stuck."

He knew he made a poor choice. He shouldn't have gone out with a group of friends who would drag him into activities that he knew were wrong. A few days later Jared was talking with Michelle about her weekend and she was extremely down. He asked why and, with tears in her eyes, she related to him what had happened to her home. Jared felt sick to his stomach because he was there when it had happened. Years down the road, those "friends" had long forgotten him and what they did that night, but he never did. He allowed people who didn't care about him to almost change the course of his life in a negative direction.

Doesn't sound very smart, does it? He allowed friends to hurt and destroy another person's sense of self-worth.

Everyone has Superficial friends. Because they can be so fun and entertaining, we end up confused and hurt when they let us down.

Superficial (Q3) friends remind us of the old legend of the Native American boy:

"...When he started to climb down a high cliff, he was asked by a rattlesnake to carry him down because it was too cold for him up so high.

> "A SUPERFICIAL (Q3) MAKES YOU THINK THAT YOU HAVE COMMON INTERESTS AND ENJOY HANGING OUT WITH EACH OTHER ONLY TO FIND OUT THAT THEY TALK BAD ABOUT YOU BEHIND YOUR BACK AND, SECRETLY, THEY CAN'T STAND YOU BECAUSE THEY'RE EITHER JEALOUS OR MENTAL."
> —ADAM, 15 YEARS OLD

When the boy asked why he should do such a thing for a snake that would likely give him a venomous and deadly bite, the snake responded that biting the boy would make no sense at all. Why would he want to bite the person who saved his life from the cold, unforgiving cliff?

Convinced, the boy carefully placed the snake into his pouch, then traversed down the dangerous rock.

After descending to the warm valley below, the boy reached in and lifted the snake out, placing him on a warm rock in the sun, but the moment he let go, the snake struck the boy with its venomous fangs, sinking them deep into his skin and releasing the poison into his body.

"OUCH!" cried the shocked boy. "Why would you do that after

Kate and Andrea had been friends since third grade; they lived just a few houses apart and their parents were friends as well. Kate decided to run for a senior student body position. She was excited about the possibility and got her friends to help with her campaign. Andrea pledged her support and helped spread the word about Kate among her classmates.

Ultimately, Kate lost what was a close election. She was crushed, but the worst part was discovering that her 'best friend' Andrea had voted for Kate's opponent. Andrea's explanation was, "The other girl was more popular. She was going to win anyway."

This disloyalty, typical of a Superficial, affected Kate's relationship with Andrea more than anything had before. Kate finally saw that while she enjoyed being around her, Andrea wasn't someone she could count on when it mattered. Unlike a True Blue, deep down, Andrea didn't want her friend to be successful—she was jealous. After this experience, Kate moved on to other friends, as did Andrea. Today, as adult women, they keep in touch and remain friends, but it's more a social friendship than one of the heart.

A woman overheard a group of her friends from their small town gossiping about another woman in the community. Like a good fly on the wall, she stayed in her spot just around the corner from the ladies, trying ever so hard to figure out whom they were talking about.

As she listened, she thought, *Geez, the lady drove them nuts!* She was too loud, too nosey, and too peculiar to put up with. The more they talked about the other lady, the more familiar she seemed, yet she still had no solid clue about whom she was until they started talking about the woman's family. She heard that the lady's husband was a professor, just like her husband. The lady had three daughters just like she did. The lady even came from the same hometown, and coincidences being coincidences, she heard that the lady was a writer, too.

She wondered who was this woman, then realized, Oh my ... it was she! She was the person of their dislike! Imagine her stomach dropping to her feet when it dawned on her that her friends were gossiping about her. Ouch. More than anything, "friends" like these cause sorrow and heartache.

the kindness I showed you?"

The snake calmly replied as it began slithering off the rock, "You knew what I was when you picked me up and put me into your pouch.""

Now, obviously a Superficial friend won't literally bite you, but some of the things a Superficial does in the name of "friendship" can come back to bite you. Generally speaking, the characteristics and behaviors of Superficials will eventually result in hurt feelings, disappointment, or distrust; it's almost unavoidable.

A SUPERFICIAL (Q3) CAN BE SELFISH

Superficials (Q3) take more from the friendship than they give. Everything revolves around them--their interests, their beliefs, their wants. They don't have as much regard for others around them as they do for themselves. Because they tend to make things all about them, you end up spending time, attention, energy, and probably money on their needs. They tend to project their negative energy onto you, while zapping your own energy.

For example, when you share some genuinely exciting news with a Superficial (Q3), she will often say something that diminishes your good news and not share your enthusiasm, or a Superficial might turn the attention to her own good news and/or successes. A true friend will always be genuinely excited with your achievements.

Superficials (Q3) rarely make an effort to build the friendship. In other words, they're the taker in the relationship—they drain you! They'll expect you to drop everything for them if disaster strikes, but probably will be slow to respond if the same thing happens to you. They're rarely there when you need them most. A real friend is there for you just as much as you're there for your friend.

These types of friends are usually not great listeners. If you bring up a problem or a challenge in your life you're experiencing, they might listen or they might not. Again, the inconsistency of Superficials (Q3) is what makes these friends unreliable. They might turn it around and one-up you and discuss their problems, their concerns.

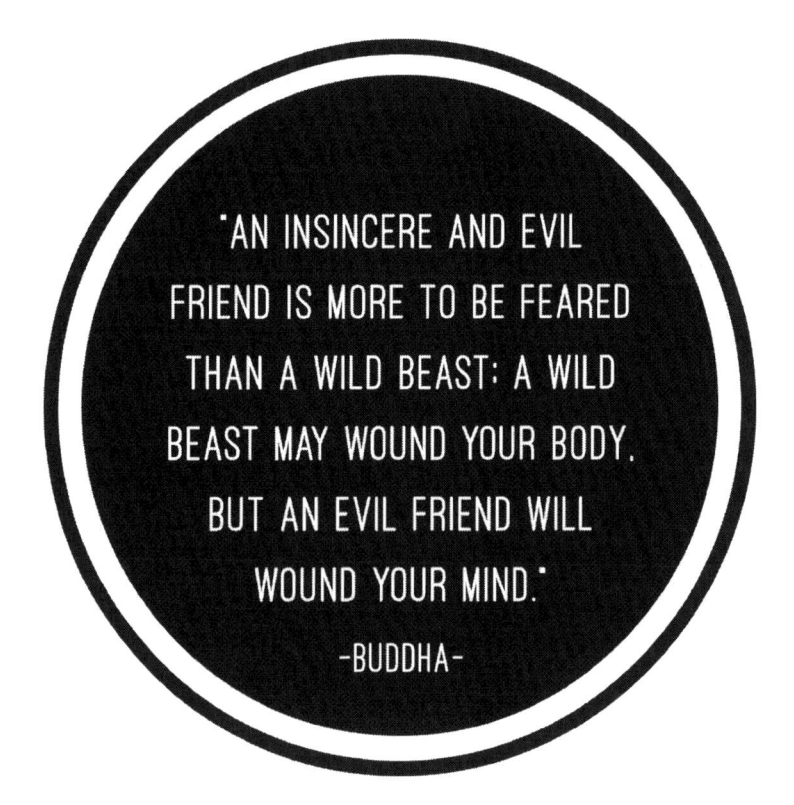

> "AN INSINCERE AND EVIL FRIEND IS MORE TO BE FEARED THAN A WILD BEAST; A WILD BEAST MAY WOUND YOUR BODY, BUT AN EVIL FRIEND WILL WOUND YOUR MIND."
>
> -BUDDHA-

FQ

When I was in high school, there was a fun dance club that all my friends went to ... well, everyone but me!

There was one night when all my friends were going. My friend suggested that I tell my parents that I was going to spend the night at her house, then I could go to the club with her.

Thank goodness I considered my parents to be True Blue (Q1) friends. I wouldn't lie to them, so I didn't go.

As it turned out, at the club that night, one of my schoolmates got into a fight and was shot and killed.

Who we associate with can be life-altering, as it unfortunately was for this particular boy.

– Kassie

The irony of selfish friends is that if you tell them you feel they're acting selfishly, they'll either be shocked and offended that you suggested such a thing or not care at all. When people are self-absorbed, they're often unaware of how they treat other people. This will cause imbalance in any relationship.

When I was in high school I became fast friends with someone I thought was a good friend. It took years to realize that this person was far from what a friend really should be. He wanted to live an edgy, exciting life that included behavior contrary to the way I was raised and the beliefs I embraced. At every turn, he would try to get me to do things that I knew ultimately wouldn't make me happy; they would only bring sadness. He always wanted to do what he wanted to do and never considered my opinion.

After high school, I tried to stay in contact with my "friend," but our lives were headed in two different directions. The lack of two-way communication would make me wonder what had happened. Did I do something wrong? Over time, I figured it out. My "friend" wasn't really a true friend. He was only looking for someone to drag down to his level. His actions were ultimately self-serving.

This was a friendship that taught me the lesson of making judgments. We're taught not to judge others, but we have to make judgments every day. Did this person really have my best interest in mind or was this person trying to bring me down? I think it's pretty easy to see what his/her true intentions were. I've watched this person from a distance over the past 25 years struggle with employment, divorce, raising a child as a single parent, drug and alcohol abuse--and these were only the things I could see from a distance.

This has been a lesson to me in the importance of selecting the right friends who will have a positive impact on me.

"I WOULD TAKE 100 REAL ENEMIES OVER ONE FAKE FRIEND ANY DAY. AT LEAST THE ENEMIES LET YOU KNOW WHERE THEY STAND AND DON'T PRETEND TO CARE."

- ANONYMOUS

GUIDE FOR RECOGNIZING SERIOUS SIGNS OF SELFISH FRIENDS:

THEY DON'T CARE ABOUT YOUR OPINIONS OR ABOUT YOUR FEELINGS.

THEY MIGHT BETRAY YOU, THEN ACT LIKE THEY DID NOTHING WRONG.

THEY PRETEND TO LISTEN, BUT AREN'T REALLY INTERESTED IN WHAT YOU HAVE TO SAY.

THEY PRETEND TO BE YOUR FRIEND BECAUSE THEY WANT SOMETHING FROM YOU.

THEY DON'T REALLY CARE ABOUT YOUR CHALLENGES OR WHAT YOU'RE GOING THROUGH.

THEY'RE MORE CONCERNED ABOUT THEMSELVES.

THEY COME UP WITH EXCUSES WHEN YOU REALLY NEED THEM.

THEY DON'T KNOW MUCH ABOUT YOUR FAMILY; IN FACT, THEY NEVER ASK.

THEY OFTEN FORGET YOUR BIRTHDAY AND OTHER IMPORTANT EVENTS.

Q3

CAN'T ALWAYS RELY ON THEM
YOU'RE DRAWN TO THEM
OFTEN WILL SEE YOU AS A FRIEND OF CONVENIENCE
WILL HAVE FUN, REGARDLESS OF THE COMPANY AROUND THEM
FREQUENTLY DISAPPOINT OTHERS
WILL ALMOST ALWAYS GO WITH THE BETTER OFFER
CAN BE MANIPULATIVE, DECEITFUL, DISHONEST, HYPERCRITICAL
CAN BE SUPERFICIAL, INSINCERE, JEALOUS, ENVIOUS
CAN BE CRITICAL AND JUDGMENTAL
USUALLY, THEY'RE NOT FORGIVING
RARELY IS ANYTHING THEIR FAULT
SELFISH -- EVERYTHING IS ABOUT THEM
THEY THRIVE ON BEING "POPULAR"
NOT SINCERE OR HONEST TO YOU OR ABOUT YOU
CAN BE TWO-FACED OR LOYAL, DEPENDS ON MOOD OR WHO'S AROUND
THEY COULD BETRAY YOU
A GOSSIP, THEY TALK BEHIND YOUR BACK -- AND OTHERS TOO
NOT DEPENDABLE, UNRELIABLE, FICKLE
THEY "LIKE" YOU FOR WHAT YOU HAVE
THEY OFTEN BEFRIEND PEOPLE ONLY WHEN IT BENEFITS THEM
YOU MAY CLICK WITH THEM IN CERTAIN SITUATIONS
YOU USUALLY HAVE IMPORTANT DIFFERENCES
IN YOUR STANDARDS AND BEHAVIORS

CHAPTER 6

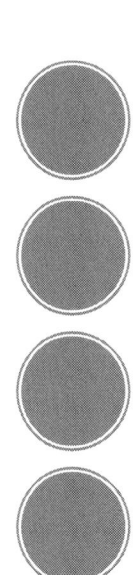

THE
STEADIES

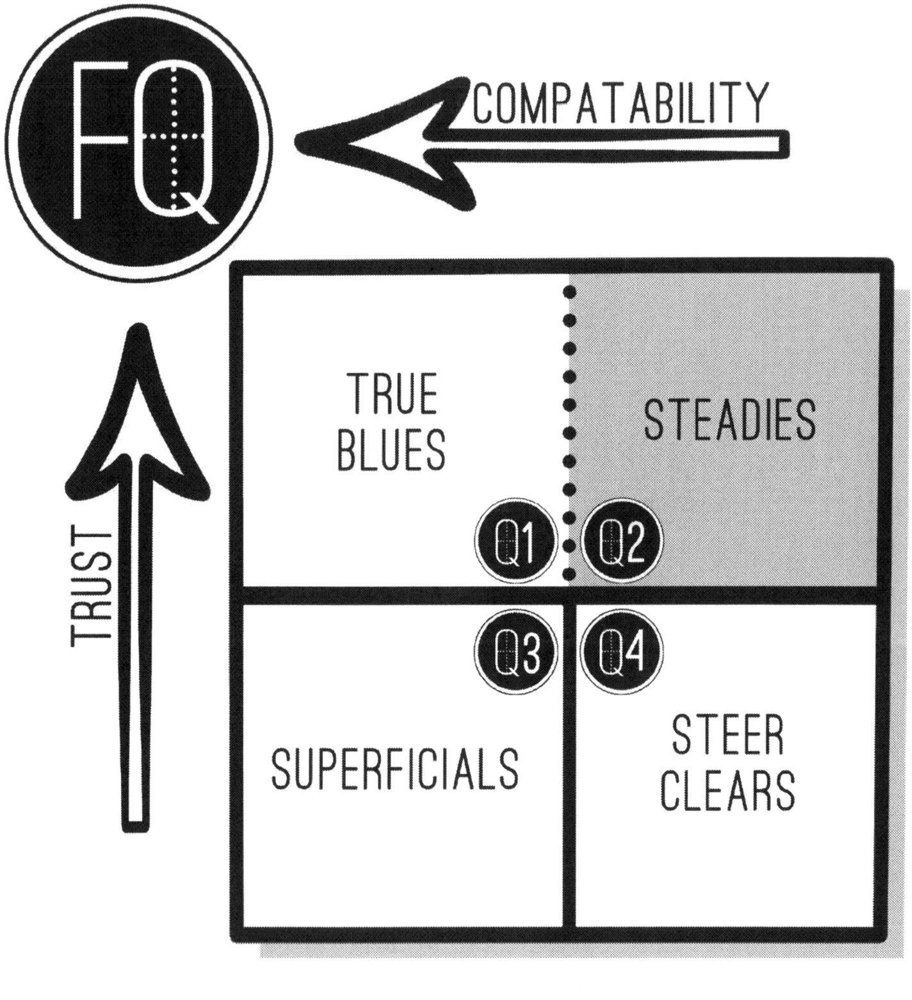
FQ
COMPATABILITY
TRUST
TRUE BLUES
STEADIES
Q1
Q2
Q3
Q4
SUPERFICIALS
STEER CLEARS

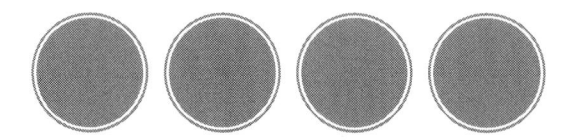

QUADRANT 2: THE STEADIES

These are the good friends in your life. You enjoy being around them and probably hang out with them often. These are friends you can always rely on, no matter what. They'll always have your back, whether you're present or not. These are the good friends who accept you for who you are --- your beliefs, values, and standards. They don't seek to compromise your standards. Most of your reliable friends are Steady (Q2) friends. You may not share a lot of the same interests or hobbies with some of them, but you find a way to still be good friends. You can't have too many Steady (Q2) friends.

Steady friends may not ultimately share all your values or beliefs, but they'll understand them, respect them, and help you honor them. It's safe for you to be with your steady friend because they won't tempt you to engage in activities that can negatively impact you.

We should treasure our good friends.

We know of two women who have been good friends since junior high school. Shauna is devout in her religion, and Amy doesn't claim a particular church; thus, Amy didn't share all of Shauna's religious convictions, but she did respect them. Throughout their junior high and high school years, Amy knew Shauna's beliefs and was supportive of her choices to live them.

As young adults, Shauna and Amy faced more complex issues such as where to live, what jobs to take, whom to date, and whom to marry. They continued to be influences for good in each other's lives. In Shauna's most difficult decisions, Amy offered support and advice that helped Shauna cling to the principles she knew to be true.

A STEADY (Q2) IS PROTECTIVE

Have you heard of an Achilles' heel?

In mythology, Peleus was the king of Greece, and Thetis was a nymph. Achilles was the son of Peleus and Thetis. When Achilles was still a baby, his mother tried to protect him from harm by dipping him into a river that had special magic water. It worked. Achilles couldn't be harmed, except for his heel where his mother had held him as she dipped him into the protective water. Now when someone is strong but has one weak spot, we call that their "Achilles' Heel."

We all have weaknesses and idiosyncrasies that someone can expose in chiding or hurtful ways. A True Blue (Q1) and a Steady (Q2) will always protect your "Achilles Heel." They would never expose nor make fun of your "Achilles Heel" in public or in a way that would hurt you. Unlike the Superficials who may have the tendency to expose, poke fun at, and talk behind your back about your weaknesses, Steady (Q2) friends value you as a person; they won't participate in such behavior.

A STEADY (Q2) IS COMFORTABLE

Friendship with a Steady is comfortable. You might not hang out a lot, but when you do see each other, there are no hurt feelings for not keeping in touch. You both understand that people are busy; however, when you're together, you focus on each other because you genuinely like each other.

We know a man who sees his friend from high school only once every few years. They live in different parts of the country and the opportunities to see each other are limited by time, distance, and expense, but when they do get together, however briefly, it's as if the intervening years don't exist. They catch up, enjoy each other's accomplishments, and renew their friendship, then go their separate ways again. Their friendship is real and has value for both of them.

A STEADY (Q2) IS FUN

You and your Steady friends have fun when you're together. You may not "click" with them like you do with your True Blues (Q1), but you enjoy being around them.

The greatest enjoyment in life comes from healthy friendships. The more Steady (Q2) friends you have, the richer and more fulfilling your life will become. You'll live your life with greater confidence because you're constantly being validated accurately as someone of great worth by those with whom you surround yourself.

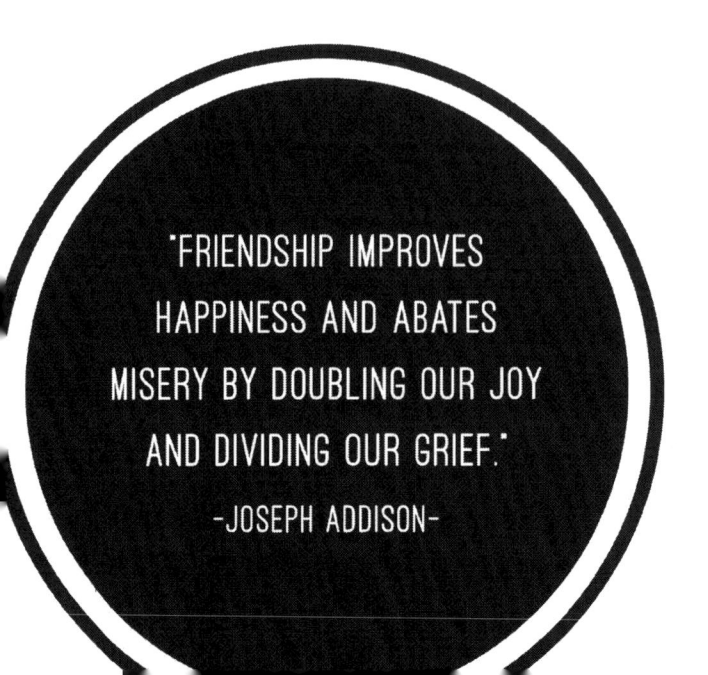

> "FRIENDSHIP IMPROVES HAPPINESS AND ABATES MISERY BY DOUBLING OUR JOY AND DIVIDING OUR GRIEF."
> -JOSEPH ADDISON-

A mom told us about her son who had a nice friend whom he would see each week at his church. They also went to scouts and school together, and were in the same carpool. These friends were comfortable around each other, but there wasn't that automatic 'click' that's felt when you're with a True Blue (Q1). Still, their son knew that if he ever needed this friend, he would be there for him.

This kid was great! He was loyal, dependable, trustworthy, and genuine. He wasn't jealous of his friend's strengths and vice versa. This friend was the first to help their son when he struggled with a project. They just didn't have that deep connection that will exist with a True Blue (Q1), and there's nothing wrong with that.

FQ

Sheila was hanging out with a Steady friend one day and he couldn't stop talking about "The Lord of the Rings." He told her that he watched the final movie in the trilogy, "The Return of the King", four times in one day. He went to the midnight showing, then watched it repeatedly all day long and late into the night. He showed her his journal that was filled with notes that he had taken each time he watched the movie with a flashlight in the dark theater, then showed her an essay that he had written about the movie.

Although she didn't share this passion for "The Lord of the Rings," she didn't judge his interest in it. She was able to appreciate him as a good friend. They saw each other at different events and she had fun when he was around, but they simply didn't connect like True Blues (Q1).

"I recently moved to Georgia. I didn't know anybody in my neighborhood. One day, my neighbor, Erika, introduced herself to me. We ran into each other frequently while going on walks.

For several months we walked together once or twice a week and talked about everyday life, but nothing deep. We were just casual acquaintances and never saw much of each other outside of our regular walks.

One day, I was completely overwhelmed, tired, and not up to my normal health. Erika brought over a piping hot, homemade, wonderfully delicious chicken pot pie meal. It sounds like such a simple gesture, but I was overwhelmed by her kindness and her selflessness. I tried to express my deep gratitude to her, but she just humbly replied that she was glad to help.

With that one gesture of giving, I realized she was a good friend, no longer just an acquaintance. A good friend is more than a person you can just walk and talk with. A good friend is someone who is giving of herself. I tried to repay her kind deed with my own acts of giving. I brought over a home-cooked dinner for her once I got better.

We then resumed our walks, and our talks became deeper, but before too long, I moved away. We still keep in touch, though. I don't think we would have maintained our friendship if she hadn't opened her heart to me and given so selflessly, thereby moving me to reciprocate, but that's why we became good friends.

I try to think of her example in other relationships with friends, knowing that giving without expecting to receive and putting another's needs ahead of your own is the true mark of a good friend."

Q2

LOYAL

SAFE

HONORABLE

RESPECTFUL

RELIABLE, DEPENDABLE

RELATIONSHIP NOT AS DEEP AS WITH A TRUE BLUE (Q1)

FUN AND ENJOYABLE

SHARE SIMILAR VALUES

PERSONALITIES MAY BE A LITTLE DIFFERENT

MUTUALLY SATISFYING RELATIONSHIP

YOU DON'T "CLICK" WITH THEM AS WELL AS A TRUE BLUE

YOU FIND VALUE IN THE RELATIONSHIP

CHAPTER 7

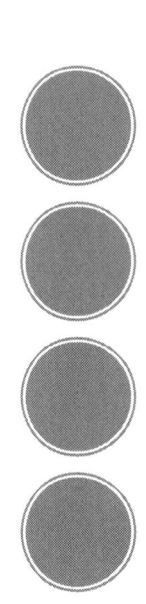

Q1

THE
TRUE BLUES

FQ ← COMPATABILITY

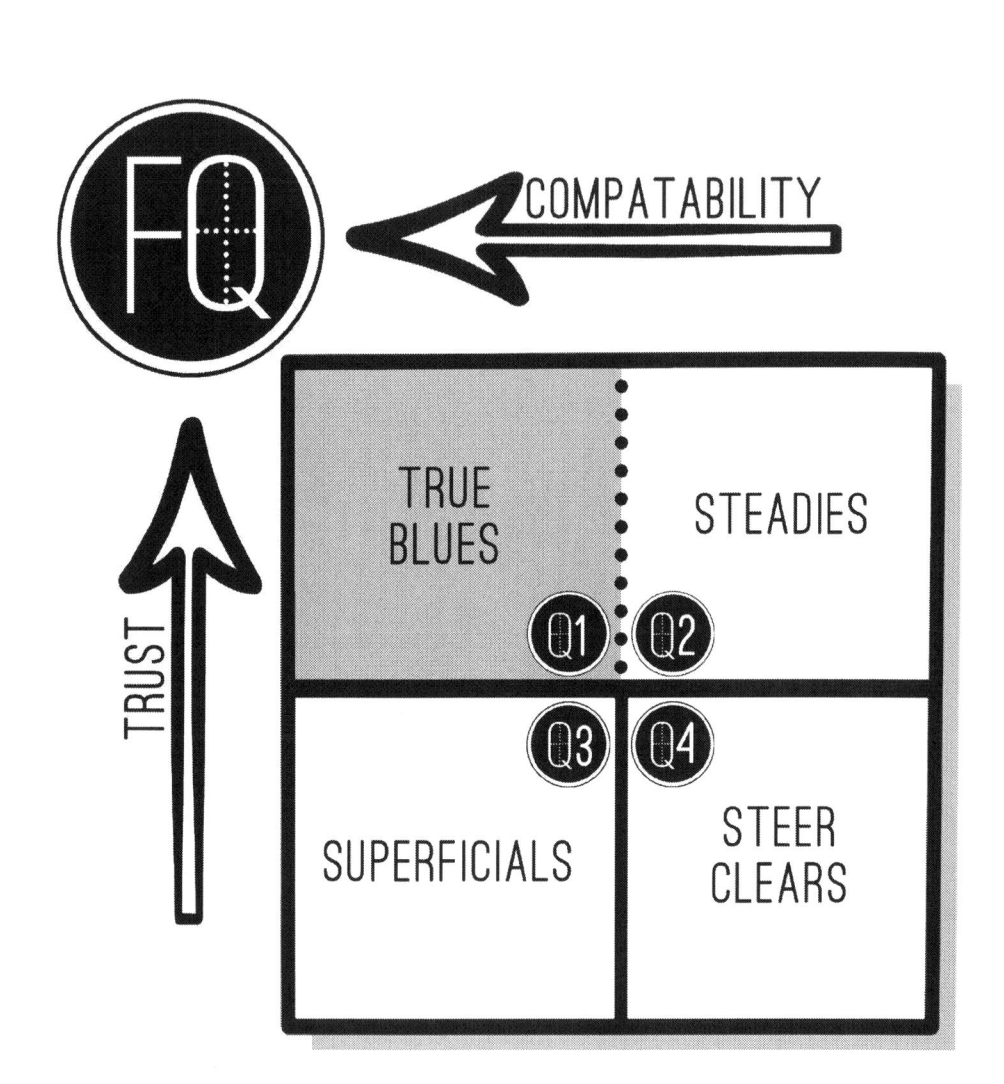

↑ TRUST

TRUE BLUES	STEADIES
Q1	Q2
Q3	Q4
SUPERFICIALS	STEER CLEARS

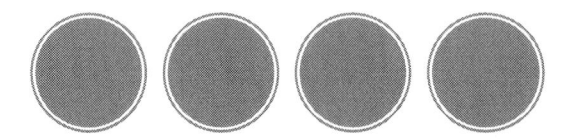

QUADRANT 1: THE TRUE BLUES

A True Blue is in the High Trust, High Compatibility quadrant. They're your "go-to" friends for everything. They're those few friends who completely understand you, connect with you, have fun with you, and rely upon you as much as you rely on them. You never have to pretend to be someone you aren't. True Blue friends are equally yoked. They're on the same level, same page and same playing field. Strive to be a True Blue (Q1) friend!

A True Blue will never ask you to be less than you should be. They love you and protect you. They honor your values. They'll strive to lift you to higher ideals and goals rather than drag you down. Choose friends who share your values so you can strengthen and encourage each other. These are the friendships you should honor and treasure. It's important that you choose them ... intentionally.

The glue that holds this sort of friendship together is the mutual respect you have for one another. You value one another as people, and you enjoy one another's company. You're his friend, not for how he can benefit you or how he can bring you gain, but simply because you like him. This is the highest form of friendship.

A TRUE BLUE (Q1) CLICKS

When you're with a True Blue (Q1), you both just "click!" You have a blast together. Laughter is common in your relationship. You're comfortable with each other. You enjoy doing many of the same things. When you have a choice, you definitely choose to spend time together. This is the type of friend you don't need any plans or special activity to have a great time. Just hanging out, talking and not doing much is still fun because you're laughing or engaging in such great conversation that time just flies when you're together. You're able to connect on so many levels.

Similar to Steady (Q2) friends, True Blues (Q1) can go long periods of time without speaking, and they never question their friendship. A True Blue is someone you always enjoy being around because you get along so well together.

"For me, "True" friends are like finding a needle in a haystack, and it takes many, many years to form these friendships. I've had only three people who would fall under this category.

"A true friend is a person who is willing to accept you for the way you are, or better yet, ones who see you for what you can become. They build you up. They don't tear you down with critical or demeaning comments.

"Friendships require "give-and-take". Friends who fall into this category for me are trustworthy, non-judgmental, understanding, and most of all unselfish (it's not always about them)."

- K. Long

When reunited after a long separation, it's easy to pick up right where you left off. You talk on the phone as if you had just spoken yesterday, regardless of how long it's been or how far away you live from each other.

When you're with a True Blue, conversation comes easily, yet when you do have a silent moment, it's relaxed and comfortable. As Dave Tyson Gentry said, "True friendship comes when silence between two people is comfortable." You can each simply be yourself whenever you're together. You never have to pretend to be someone different when you're with a True Blue (Q1).

A TRUE BLUE (Q1) IS RELIABLE

When you need help, your True Blue friend offers it; when your True Blue friend needs help, you provide it. Because we can rely on them explicitly, this friend provides a safe harbor at all times.

Think about a harbor. A harbor is a refuge from the storm out on the sea. Ships do everything they can to get into harbor to avoid the dangers and troubles of a raging sea. A True Blue is that safe harbor. He provides safety and shelter from the storm of life's realities, whether it be at home, school, or work.

The Greek drama of

> "FRIENDSHIP IS THE INEXPRESSIBLE COMFORT OF FEELING SAFE WITH A PERSON, HAVING NEITHER TO WEIGH THOUGHTS NOR MEASURE WORDS."
> —GEORGE ELIOT—

FRIENDSHIP QUADRANT

Damon and Pythias is a great example of a True Blue (Q1) friendship.

Damon and Pythias were two friends in ancient Greece who lived in the city-state of Syracuse. Dionysius, the dictator who ruled the city, had condemned Pythias to die. Damon knew that Pythias' mother was a widow and his sister was unmarried. Damon went to Pythias and told him he would take his place in prison so Pythias could travel to his mother's home and make arrangements for his family's well-being in advance of his death.

At first Pythias refused, but Damon insisted, even though he knew that if Pythias didn't return in time that he would be the one executed. Finally, Pythias relented and Damon took his place in the prison cell, with Pythias swearing to return in time. Pythias quickly traveled to his homeland and saw to the needs of his mother and sister. He then told them goodbye and left to keep his word to his friend, Damon.

In his journey back to Syracuse, he was attacked by thieves, who stole his belongings and left him tied to a tree. After hours of struggle, he finally freed himself and again set off to reach his friend and prevent Damon's death. Taking no time to nurse his wounds, he then encountered a raging stream swollen from a recent storm. There was no safe way to cross. Risking his life, Pythias crossed the stream, then, reaching the hot, dry desert, he was forced to struggle across it in his injured state. Driven by his love for his friend, he continued on until he finally arrived in Syracuse.

Rushing to the place of execution, he intercepted Damon as the guards led him to his death. Pythias threw his arms around his friend, pleading for forgiveness for his late arrival. Damon, who was prepared to die, quickly became sorrowful, realizing that his brave friend would now die instead.

The tyrant, Dionysius, who had come to witness the execution, observed the amazing act of love and friendship between these two friends. He was moved with compassion and released them both to their freedom.

A TRUE BLUE (Q1) IS LOYAL

True Blues are loyal at all times. They will keep your confidences. They always "have your back," even when you're not around to defend yourself. It's comforting to know that this friend is always looking out for you.

You might think, if you're about to make a poor decision, True Blue friends will look the other way and not say anything to stop you. Nothing could be further from the truth. If they believe that your behavior is foolish, dangerous, or will lead to problems, a True Blue will show loyalty by having the courage to communicate it to you, even if it means risking you becoming angry or offended. It takes courage to be a real friend. Fear, on the other hand, can deprive you of lasting friendships.

Some people aren't true friends because of their unwillingness to be a real friend under all circumstances. Some of us think a true friend will always accept us for who we are regardless of how we act, even if it's foolish. A true friend will help us make positive changes regardless of the immediate consequences.

For example, a habit of lying and deceiving will only bring sadness. If you engage in a negative behavior like this, your True

Blue will have the courage to tell you to stop it. A True Blue (Q1) won't condone behavior that ultimately hurts you or others around you.

'IT TAKES A GREAT DEAL OF COURAGE TO STAND UP TO YOUR ENEMIES, BUT A GREAT DEAL MORE TO STAND UP TO YOUR FRIENDS.'

—PROFESSOR DUMBLEDORE

J.K. ROWLING, HARRY POTTER AND THE SORCERER'S STONE

A TRUE BLUE (Q1) IS TRUSTWORTHY

You trust them in every way. This type of friend doesn't lie to you. You may have people, even family members, in your life whom you love, but because of a poor choice that they've made, you don't trust them anymore. **If a friend can't be trusted, he can't be a True Blue (Q1).**

George MacDonald, a Scottish author, poet, and Christian minister in the 1800's, said, "To be trusted is a greater compliment than being loved."

Since your True Blues aren't jealous of you, you can trust them to give you honest counsel when it comes to education, relationships, career, and other important life decisions.

When we're young we often think we have a 'best friend,' but if this person's choices consistently hurt us, then she isn't a 'best friend.' True Blues are the same reliable friend yesterday, today, and tomorrow. Their status and your feelings toward them remain constant from day to day. In general, we feel 100% safe with our True Blue friends.

A TRUE BLUE (Q1) IS ACCEPTING

True Blues accept you and love you in spite of your faults or quirks. Yes, they help you overcome your weaknesses, but you know they love and accept you despite your imperfections. You both accept each other for exactly who you are. You can completely be yourself with this person. There are no pretenses. Their genuine interest in you means they're good listeners, which is a trait often missing in so-called 'friends.' They appreciate you and actually embrace what makes you different from them. They know that they can learn from you, and they never take you for granted.

They're sincerely interested in you and your successes. In some cases, they know your weaknesses better than you do. They understand how hard it can be to change, so they're patient when it comes to your failings and your attempts to change.

A TRUE BLUE (Q1) IS ENCOURAGING

A True Blue (Q1) will inspire you, motivate you, and encourage you. They lift, empathize, and support each other continually. They'll help you become your best self.

There will be times in your life when you need to be lifted up, and True Blues (Q1) will be able to do that in just the right way for you. They are thrilled for your successes. They celebrate your victories with as much enthusiasm as you do. They're proud of your achievements and enjoy what makes you unique. They can do this because they understand that your successes don't diminish their own value as a person.

True Blues (Q1) fill you with a certain confidence, or self-belief, that allows you to achieve greater things in your life. They're genuinely interested in you, as you are in them. They like you for who you are, not for what you have, or who you know. Most important, they encourage you in the right things, never asking you to compromise your personal standards and values.

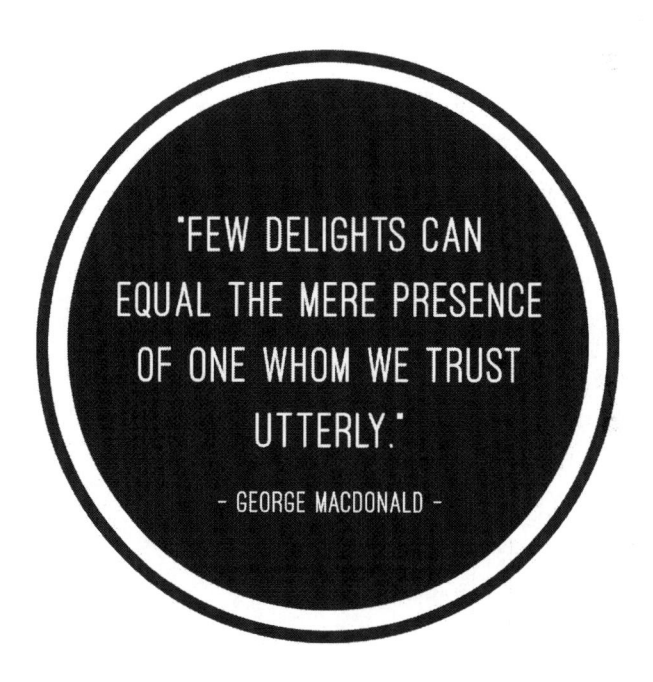

> "FEW DELIGHTS CAN EQUAL THE MERE PRESENCE OF ONE WHOM WE TRUST UTTERLY."
> — GEORGE MACDONALD —

A TRUE BLUE (Q1) IS FORGIVING

True Blues will quickly and frankly forgive. This means when you make a mistake they won't hold a grudge. Once forgiveness is given, the incident isn't brought up or used against you in the future.

> A TRUE BLUE (Q1) HAS THE RARE ABILITY TO HELP YOU BECOME BETTER WHILE, AT THE SAME TIME, APPRECIATING YOU FOR WHO YOU ARE.

True friends will usually feel sorry for their error in judgment and ask their friend to forgive them. If you can forgive your friends when they make a mistake, you'll more likely be able to save the friendship. Let's face it, we all make mistakes.

The real test of a friendship is what happens when you've been wronged. This is especially true if a friend doesn't think they need to ask you for forgiveness. We once had a close friend do something that hurt us. We needed a resolution. At the very least, we wanted a sincere apology before we could forgive and move on. We received neither, so we chose forgiveness anyway. It wasn't easy, but we're so glad that we did. By choosing to frankly forgive this friend, we freed ourselves from the burden of anger. Also, we've seen the friendship with that person grow far beyond what it was. Life wouldn't be as sweet and rewarding as it is today without that friendship.

There may come a time when you may be the one who needs to be forgiven. Fortunately for Q1's, they're willing to forgive each other when necessary.

There's a great line in the movie "Shrek" where Donkey follows Shrek back to his home. Shrek asks Donkey why he's still following him if he's so disappointed in him for not wanting to help Princess Fiona. Donkey replies, "Because that's what friends do. They forgive each other!"

A TRUE BLUE (Q1) IS SIMILAR

True Blue friends share the same or similar behaviors, standards, and beliefs as you. Essentially, you have the same value system. You would never ask your friends to lower their standards. If your values include honesty, kindness, loyalty, patience, etc. then their values are the same.

Having these similar values regarding important life choices helps create the all-important trust between True Blues. As you've previously learned, Superficials (Q3) and Steer Clears (Q4) can't be trusted in this same way. Remember, these two quadrants are "Below the Line of Trust." At some point in life, everyone is tempted or pressured to change.

In the classic film "It's a Wonderful Life," The main character, George Bailey, thinks the world would be a better place if he had not been born. He believes he hasn't made a difference in the world.

Clarence, the Angel, visits George and shows him how his family, friends, and the town itself would have turned out if he had indeed not been born.

At the end of this classic movie Clarence leaves a truthful inscription in a book that he gives to George: "Remember, George, no man is a failure who has friends."

FRIENDSHIP QUADRANT

> "A FRIEND IS ONE TO WHOM ONE MAY POUR OUT ALL THE CONTENTS OF ONE'S HEART, CHAFF AND GRAIN TOGETHER, KNOWING THAT THE GENTLEST OF HANDS WILL TAKE AND SIFT IT, KEEP WHAT IS WORTH KEEPING, AND WITH THE BREATH OF KINDNESS BLOW THE REST AWAY."
>
> —ARABIAN PROVERB

Superficials (Q3) may pressure you to change your positive behaviors for negative ones, but True Blues (Q1) don't apply this type of peer pressure--ever! By doing so, they wouldn't be true to themselves, and they wouldn't be true to your friendship.

True Blues (Q1) are the type of friends who encourage you to make choices consistent with your positive value system. They're like a compass; they help point you in the right direction, but it's always left up to you to choose your own path.

Of course, it may not always be as black and white as this. After all, we already spoke about how a Q1 helps you become better. What we want to emphasize is that you and a True Blue share similar values and behaviors in what matters most.

> "WHEN A FRIEND DOES SOMETHING WRONG, DON'T FORGET ALL THE THINGS THEY DID RIGHT."
>
> - ANONYMOUS -

We have few True Blue (Q1) friendships in our lives because they take time and effort to cultivate. Some of you may only have one or, two True Blue (Q1) friends. Maybe you don't have one right now.

Recall Terri's story? She was a teenager who was a leader in her high school, but she was still unable to find a Q1 outside her immediate family until she went to college. True Blue (Q1) friendships should be treasured. Some people search for years to find an individual who fits the description of a True Blue friend. Don't give up hope; keep searching!

Just because you don't have a True Blue doesn't mean you have to be alone. Take it as an opportunity to explore relationships with your Steady (Q2) friends and all those people you still don't know. Sometimes you may be so desperate to have a True Blue that you may be tempted to change yourself and your standards so that a Superficial will accept you. You then deceive yourself by pretending to think that the Superficial is actually your True Blue. By doing so, you are only setting yourself up for disappointment.

"MY FATHER ALWAYS USED TO SAY THAT WHEN YOU DIE, IF YOU'VE GOT FIVE REAL FRIENDS, THEN YOU'VE HAD A GREAT LIFE."

–LEE IACOCCA

"A TRUE FRIEND NEVER GETS IN YOUR WAY UNLESS YOU HAPPEN TO BE GOING DOWN."

- ARNOLD H. GLASGOW -

Q1

A BEST FRIEND
YOU HAVE A NATURAL CONNECTION
SHARE COMMON INTERESTS
SIMILAR BEHAVIORS
SUPPORTIVE
FORGIVING
LOYAL; A CONFIDANT
THEY SHARE WILLINGLY
DEPENDABLE, RELIABLE
DEFENDS YOU AND STANDS UP FOR YOU
THEY HAVE YOUR BACK; THEY DON'T TALK BEHIND IT
TRUSTWORTHY, HONEST WITH YOU AND ABOUT YOU
CAN TELL YOU WHEN YOU'RE WRONG, WITHOUT HURTING YOUR FEELINGS
YOU HAVE FUN WHEN YOU'RE WITH EACH OTHER
SINCERE; THEY HAVE A GENUINE INTEREST IN YOU
THEY LOVE YOU DESPITE YOUR FAULTS
ACCEPT YOU FOR WHO YOU ARE
HELP YOU BECOME A BETTER PERSON
THEY'RE SELFLESS, WILLING TO HELP YOU ANY TIME
THEY'RE GENUINELY HAPPY FOR YOUR SUCCESSES
THEY ENCOURAGE, LIFT AND HELP YOU BE BETTER
MORALLY COURAGEOUS
YOU REALLY CLICK WITH THEM
YOU SHARE THE SAME VALUES AND STANDARDS

CHAPTER 8

LIVING THE FRIENDSHIP QUADRANT

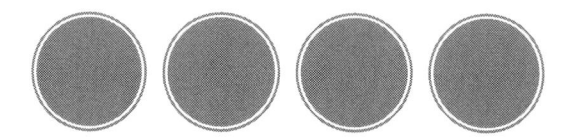

LIVING THE FRIENDSHIP QUADRANT

Once you've learned the principles of the Friendship Quadrant it's important to apply them correctly on a continual basis. Often, it's easy to identify where certain friends are in the FQ model. Other times, it's extremely difficult because you have to dig deep and analyze yourself and your friendships. It's important to be completely honest as you use this tool to assess and apply the principles of the Friendship Quadrant. If you're truly honest, you may be surprised at some of the quadrants in which you place your friends. It's hard to analyze friends and admit that some just aren't the friends you want them to be. This doesn't mean you cast people aside, but recognize that some friends are better for you than others, and you need to be able to tell which is which.

One of our dear friends told us that she advised her teenagers to always take a 'wingman' along when they went out with friends.

WINGMAN - *[wing-man] noun: A pilot whose plane is positioned behind and outside the leader in a formation of flying aircraft; someone who helps or supports another; a friend or close associate.*

A good wingman helps you see things that you may not see on your own, he will protect you.

Why can a lion take down a healthy elephant that's at least eight times bigger than it is? Sure, the lion's "King of the Jungle" attitude definitely helps, but it's mostly because of the fact that lions run in a pride, which is a large family grouping. There's strength in numbers, so stick with your friends who are "Above the Line of Trust"-- your True Blue (Q1) and your Steady (Q2) friends -- and you'll be protected. If you choose to go somewhere alone with a Superficial (Q3) friend, it may be great fun ... until she chooses to participate in a behavior that goes against what you know is right.

An important note: People **_can_** change. That's one of the main tenants of the Friendship Quadrant! You're not etched in stone. You can change and so can your friends. But when evaluating your friends, learn to be intentional with the choices you make so you can protect yourself and your future.

Warning: If you have friends who exhibit Superficial (Q3) behaviors and you decide to simply exclude them, you may do tremendous harm to them. Instead, challenge your Superficial (Q3) friends to change their behavior. You need to have the courage to challenge others to change for the better. You may do this simply by setting the right example and saying "no" when invited to participate in activities or behaviors you know are wrong.

Once you recognize that someone behaves like a Superficial (Q3), don't shun him. Instead, invite him to activities with you and your "Above the Line of Trust" friends. This will allow your friend the opportunity to step up and get "Above the Line of Trust" himself.

As stated previously, the Friendship Quadrant isn't a tool of exclusion. You can spend a lot of time with a Superficial (Q3). People can change and can move from one quadrant to another. Allow this to happen, but be cautious and wise about it so you don't get hurt. The Friendship Quadrant is a tool to protect yourself, manage expectations, enrich current friendships, and become a better friend. Having said this, remember this guideline: **Be careful WHERE you go with a Superficial (Q3) and NEVER be alone with a Steer Clear (Q4).**

Being alone with the wrong friend can put you in harmful, hurtful, and sometimes helpless situations that you don't want to be in. Again, this doesn't mean exclusion or being rude and mean; it means you need to have an awareness of the situations around you and use this tool to guide your choices.

Do you travel through your life telling yourself, "If I keep going long enough, I'm going to get somewhere," yet you never clearly define exactly what or where that place is?

More importantly, with regard to your friends, do you travel

"In her junior year of high school, Kathy was invited to go out with a group of friends. They picked her up and drove downtown. The later the night, the crazier the friends became. They put themselves in dangerous situations, and Kathy was stuck. (This was before cell phones if you can imagine!) She asked if they could take her home, but they said they weren't done having fun. Home was forty minutes away.

When they finally dropped her off, it was 2:00 am and her parents were worried, needless to say! She vowed that night to always be the driver so she would be in control. She also decided that going out with a group of Superficials (Q3) without a plan was a poor decision!"

through your life not really paying any attention to who you're traveling through life with? If you randomly choose your friends and don't care about who or what types of people you spend time with, then your path will be long, tiring, rough, and at times, even dangerous.

In Lewis Carroll's *Alice in Wonderland,* Alice asks the Cheshire Cat, "Would you please tell me which way I ought to go from here?" The Cheshire Cat replies, "That depends a great deal on where you want to go."

Alice says, "I admit, I don't much care where."

> BE INTENTIONAL ABOUT WHERE YOU WANT TO GO. BE INTENTIONAL ABOUT CHOOSING WHO YOU WANT TO GO WITH.

The Cheshire Cat then says, "Then it doesn't really matter much which way you go, does it?"

"Just so I get somewhere," responds Alice.

The Cheshire Cat says something profound: "Oh, you're sure to get there if you keep walking long enough!"

Going through life and choosing Superficials (Q3) as friends, reminds us of Alice at this stage of her life. She doesn't know where she's going. Picking friends at random, she struggles throughout the entire story as she gets into one mess after another.

Your friendship choices have long-term consequences--and they aren't trivial. Who you hang out with says a lot about who you are, even if you don't feel that's a fair assessment. Sometimes teenagers will say the following: "I'm not like them; I just like hanging out with them. They're nice to me. I'm part of the group. They know I don't do that stuff. I'm still me. I haven't changed." Sadly, people will judge you based on the friends you choose. The phrase "Guilty by Association" applies in this scenario. Not only can this impact you in the short term, it can negatively impact you with future jobs and future family.

Consider this example: It's Saturday night. A group of friends are at a fun party. Everything is going great. You see tons of your friends from school. You notice that the majority of the group starts doing things they shouldn't. They all start to smoke marijuana and do other drugs.

You stay strong to your values and standards and decline the many invitations to join in on the "fun." You're feeling pretty good about yourself for maintaining your values, and inside you look forward to reporting back to your parents that they were wrong about the bad influence this group of friends can have.

All of a sudden, you hear loud noises. People start yelling and running. You turn to your left and you see kids hopping over fences. You turn to your right and see kids running out of the back yard. Still clueless as to what's going on, you turn around and straight ahead you see fifteen police officers gathering all the drugs as well as corralling all the remaining kids at the party. You begin to panic, but it's too late to react. The nearest officer grabs you and escorts you inside. You feel it's still okay because you didn't do anything wrong--you didn't smoke nor do the drugs.

A few moments later you hear the words, "Everyone line up against the wall." You do so. Your heartbeat begins to increase rapidly as you witness what's taking place. The officers are smelling the hands and clothes of each person. If they smell marijuana, they're arrested. If not, they're let go. Unfortunately, you were around it all night with your "friends," some of whom were able to escape, and you notice that the smell is all over you.

It's your turn. The officer approaches you and smells you. He instructs the officer to his left to book you. You begin to panic and claim that you didn't smoke marijuana nor do the drugs, that it's all one big mistake, but it falls on deaf ears. You're guilty by association. This will negatively impact college and job applications...and you didn't even do anything wrong. You're innocent, but there's no way to prove it.

The deeper question of this scenario is why did this teenager want to be there? What was the draw? What was he doing there in the first place? Why was he wanting to be around those types of 'friends'? Who you associate with says a lot about who you are and what you value. Hopefully, if you had been with a True Blue (Q1) or a Steady (Q2) you wouldn't have felt the pull to stay at the party with the Superficials (Q3). Remember, there's strength in numbers when you are with friends who are "Above the Line of Trust."

Two combined influences are always stronger than two separate influences. There was a study done to measure the pulling power of horses. It showed that one horse could pull about 2,500 pounds by itself. The test was repeated several times, then a test was done using two horses yoked together. One would expect that the horses could pull double the weight, about 5,000 pounds, right? Wrong! Two horses working together pulled 12,500 pounds. That's five times the amount that one horse could pull alone. This principle applies to friendships.

When you're working together with your friends, you're like two horses pulling a common load. You can do so much more together than you could ever do alone, as long as you're "Above the Line of Trust".

Make it your goal to not only become a True Blue (Q1) friend to someone, but to also surround yourself with as many friends as possible who are "Above the Line of Trust" (Q1 & Q2 friends)! The more True Blues and Steadies you surround yourself with, the stronger you'll become!

TIME FOR A PARADIGM SHIFT

A king once had a boulder placed on a roadway, then he hid himself and watched to see if anyone would remove the huge rock. Some of the king's wealthiest merchants and courtiers came by and simply walked around it. Many loudly blamed the king for not keeping the roads clear, but none did anything about getting the big stone out of the way.

A peasant came along carrying a load of vegetables. On approaching the boulder, the peasant laid down his burden and tried to move the stone to the side of the road.

STAY ABOVE SALT THE LINE OF TRUST

After much pushing and straining, he finally succeeded. As the peasant picked up his load of vegetables, he noticed a purse lying in the road where the boulder had been. The purse contained many gold coins and a note from the king indicating that the gold was for the person who removed the boulder from the roadway. The peasant learned what many people never understand; every obstacle presents an opportunity.

If you have realized that either you or a friend is a Superficial ... remember this: People can change and YOU can help them do it!

CASE IN POINT

Once out of reform school, Bill Sands set out to get even with his father, his mother, the reform school, and society in general. In July of 1941, he was sentenced and sent to San Quentin Prison. He soon became a hardened, hate-filled convict. Once, he even tried to kill a fellow prisoner and nearly succeeded. He spent many weeks in solitary confinement planning his revenge on society.

PARADIGM - [par-uh-dahym] noun: A set of assumptions, concepts, values, and practices that constitutes a way of viewing reality for thecommunity that shares them, especially in an intellectual discipline.)

Considering his record of incorrigibility, his chances for enjoying freedom in society again seemed slim; however, the new warden at San Quentin changed his life. Clinton T. Duffy was a man who believed prisoners could change.

A radio commentator once said to Warden Duffy, "You should know that leopards don't change their spots!" Duffy replied, "You should know I don't work with leopards. I work with men, and men change every day."

With Warden Duffy's encouragement, Bill did change, won his parole, and became a respectable citizen. Within a few years he was married, had a comfortable home, drove a nice car, and was a popular nightclub entertainer.

There was a time, when I was younger, that I wasn't ready to be a True Blue (Q1), so I kept myself in the Superficial (Q3) category. I was simply too immature or unsure of myself to be a good or true friend.

I'm probably the perfect example of why you shouldn't shun a Superficial (Q3), because often they're simply trying to find themselves, and in the process they look like a Superficial (Q3), yet have the potential to be a Steady or a True Blue.

I love that the Friendship Quadrant encourages "inclusion" of the Superficial (Q3) with the simple warning to always make sure you have at least one True Blue (Q1) or Steady (Q2) with you. Because I was invited along by these good friends, I eventually changed my selfish behavior and became a Steady and a True Blue myself.

As stated earlier, once you understand the basic concepts of the Friendship Quadrant (FQ), it's important to understand how to apply them in a positive way. FQ is designed to empower you with wisdom to make successful decisions about your friends and relationships. The Friendship Quadrant isn't about labeling others; it's about helping you choose your friends wisely and seeking to improve yourself. There's a distinct difference.

To live the Friendship Quadrant, you must make a conscious choice. It's intentional. It's deliberate. There should be a sense of accountability and responsibility in the decision of whom to spend your time with on a daily basis. Remember, there's a difference between making a ***judgment*** and ***being judgmental***.

One of our good friends likes to say, "Live deliberately!"

To "Live Deliberately" means knowing why you're doing what you're doing. Live your life with purpose. Know who your friends truly are and why they're your friends.

The phrase "live deliberately" is appealing because it means choosing the elements of your life based on what you value. This brings more authenticity into your life. If you're deliberately seeking positive influences, you won't be concerned if that person is well connected or "popular." You'll only seek friendships with people who motivate you to grow and with whom you genuinely enjoy spending time. Remember the example of "Alice in Wonderland." Her lack of "living deliberately" got her into trouble.

The Friendship Quadrant is a tool. It helps you discover what quadrant your friends fit into, as well as what type of friend you are.

Just like any other tool, if used incorrectly, it can be harmful. Use this tool with wisdom and care. Again, the Friendship Quadrant is about inclusion, not exclusion. You should take every reasonable opportunity to include Superficials (Q3) with you and your other Q1's or Q2's in activities. One of the worst feelings in the world is the feeling of rejection. As long as your Superficial (Q3) friends' behavior is positive, then by all means include them. Often Superficials (Q3) will actually make positive changes simply because you included them and showed them how true and good friends treat each other.

This is actually how a Superficial (Q3) can eventually become a True Blue (Q1) or a Steady (Q2). Over time, you may have friends who move from one quadrant to another. Hopefully none of your True Blues will leave that quadrant, but it's possible. It's also reasonable for a Superficial (Q3) to move up to a Steady (Q2) or even a True Blue (Q1). It's amazing when you watch someone who begins as a Superficial (Q3) and, over time, becomes a True Blue (Q1)!

TIME TO PUT PRINCIPLES INTO PRACTICE

On a separate piece of paper, respond to the following questions:

1) Write down all the friends you can think of (school, clubs, church, teams, organizations, etc.).

2) Identify where you believe your friends belong in the Friendship Quadrant.

3) Write down what you've learned while doing this exercise. What shocked/surprised you? How satisfied are you with your results?

4) Write down what you plan to do/change with regard to those friendships.

"WHEN THE WEAK ARE MADE STRONG,
AND THE STRONG BECOME STRONGER THROUGH
OUR ASSOCIATION, FRIENDSHIP IS REAL."

-ANONYMOUS

CHAPTER 9

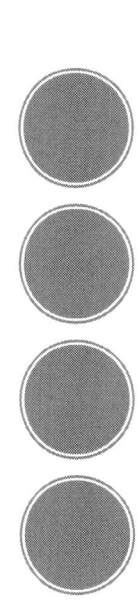

WHAT KIND
OF FRIEND ARE YOU?

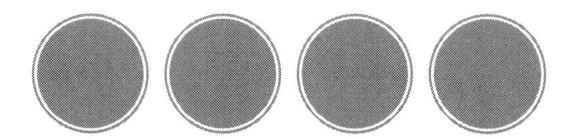

WHAT KIND OF FRIEND ARE YOU?

Now, let's focus on you. What kind of friend are you? You know that you can't be a True Blue (Q1) friend to everyone. As stated earlier, it simply takes too much time and effort to cultivate the closeness of that type of friendship; plus, you simply can't force the "click" factor. You can, however, be a Steady (Q2) friend to many people.

How do you accomplish this? First, understand that you can't force a friendship. If you feel like you don't have a lot of friends, ask yourself if you have behaviors and attributes like those "Above the Line of Trust" (Q1 & Q2).

Are you a loyal, unselfish, encouraging, and fun friend? Are you trustworthy? Are you kind? Or, be honest; do you get jealous easily? Do you make fun of your friends? Are you more concerned about being popular than being a good friend? The answers to these questions will determine if you have some changes you need to make to become a good and/or better friend.

Strive to be an "Oh there you are!" type person instead of a "Here I am" person! Think outward, not inward. Think about what your friends need to be happy. What concerns them? What makes them smile? What makes them forget their stresses and worries? When you can forget yourself and genuinely become interested in other people, you will be happier. This will help you be a better friend to others.

> "YOU CAN MAKE MORE FRIENDS IN TWO MONTHS BY BECOMING INTERESTED IN OTHER PEOPLE THAN YOU CAN IN TWO YEARS BY TRYING TO GET OTHER PEOPLE INTERESTED IN YOU."
> —DALE CARNEGIE

ASK QUESTIONS

If you ask a lot of questions of new friends from the very beginning, they'll see it as a sign that you're interested in them and their life. This will indicate to them that you're not someone who merely thinks selfishly.

LISTEN

Be an effective listener. After you ask questions, truly listen to the answers given. Don't just show you're interested; be interested. The more interested you are in others, the more they'll be interested in you. People can tell when you're sincerely listening to them or if you're distracted.

Where are your eyes focused? On the person speaking or the people around them? Be sincere. Nod. Be engaged in the conversation. Respond to the things they're saying.

The less you say and the more you listen, the more they'll say. The more they say, the more they open up. The more they open up, the stronger the connection. The stronger the connection, the deeper the friendship. They may begin to open up and confide in you, and you may be able to help them in ways nobody else ever could.

TOP 10 TIPS TO LISTENING EFFECTIVELY

When friends begin to open up and discuss personal and private things, do the following:

1. Withhold the temptation to speak and offer advice.
2. Just listen.
3. Say, "What else?"
4. Validate the things they're saying.
5. Show empathy and compassion (put yourself in their shoes).
6. Keep saying "What else?" until they say they're done. Ask clarifying questions that will help them in their thought process.
7. Don't be afraid of silence. Don't break the silence because you're uncomfortable or feel awkward. Often they're thinking or feeling deeply, which means they have more to say.

8. Don't offer advice or an opinion unless they ask for it. Often people just want to be heard.
9. Don't look at, respond to, or answer your phone. Put it on silent.
10. Just love them. Don't have an agenda.

OBSERVE

Be observing. Watch the people in your school whom you most respect. (Not the most popular, but the most respected.) What do they do? How do they take care of themselves? How do they treat others? Perhaps you could try to adopt some of these qualities as your own. If you do, you'll eventually become and attract that type of person.

Remember, the goal isn't to have more friends, but to have "quality" friends of high standards. Look for friends who make you want to be better and then be sure you're that kind of friend, too.

BE KIND

Regardless of how others treat you, you can always treat others with kindness and dignity.

Be careful about teasing your friends. Although at many times it may be tempting, exercise self-discipline. While you may consider it just horseplay or funny, they may see it as demeaning and lacking in respect for them. If you're constantly teasing and using sarcasm, your friends won't confide in you when they have something serious to talk about.

Not only that, but you may not know what they are currently

> **THE ROOT WORD IN SARCASM IS SARCI, WHICH MEANS "TEARING OF THE FLESH."**

going through in life. They may have a low self-esteem. Their parents may be contemplating a divorce or always fighting. They may be emotionally or physically abused at home or by others. They may be struggling in school. They may have a learning disability.

Don't add to the fire. When people are teased, rarely do they just "shrug it off." Many times they internalize it, which impacts them in a deeper way than most people realize. They become self-conscious of everything that they're teased about. Be strong enough to become a beacon of light. Be known for being kind and for standing up for others. Elevate and protect others. You may be the only person in your friend's life who is kind. Be someone he can trust. Can you trust someone who makes fun of you and isn't kind? Those who are kind are rarely "Below the Line of Trust." Stay Above the Line of Trust.

DON'T BE DEMANDING

Avoid being demanding. A great friendship is not about dumping all of your problems into it. It requires give and take. Trust can be difficult to establish if you are constantly needy and demanding too much time, comfort, support, or reassurance. If you are this way, you run the risk of others not wanting to be around you.

BE NON-JUDGMENTAL

Be non-judgmental. Judging your friends won't help them to trust you. Initially they may find your "advice" helpful but after a while, when your friends realize you always think you know what's best for them, they'll be less inclined to come to you with any confidences. Instead, treat your friends with respect. Listen to their confidences in a supportive and non-judgmental way. Attempt to give them your unconditional support, unless they are going to do something that is harmful to themselves or others.

Motivational speaker and author John Bytheway shared the following insight. Envision a tandem bicycle. The people on the bike are either pedalers (Q1's & Q2's), coasters, or brakers (Q3's & Q4's).

The Pedalers encourage others and have a positive attitude. These are the friends who look outside themselves and focus on helping others.

The Coasters focus on themselves. They neither hurt nor help the others. They are selfishly enjoying the ride.

The Brakers actually hold everyone back and stop any progression. They inhibit the others from moving forward. They continually put others down or are "stirring the pot" by creating controversy via gossip or outright criticism and sarcasm.

Be a pedaler! Surround yourself with pedalers. You'll get to your destination much faster than if you were pedaling alone. It's easier to pedal the "uphills" of life when you're surrounded by those who are pedaling all around you.

Now that we've discussed what kind of friend you should be, it's time for some self-reflection.

What kind of friend are you? Are you a True Blue? Steady? Superficial? Steer Clear? Are you trustworthy? Are you "Above or Below the Line of Trust?" Do others rely on you? Do they confide in you? Are you honest? Are you fiercely loyal? Are you fake? Do you go with what's most popular? Do you make fun of other people, especially those closest to you, even if you are "just kidding"? Are you selfish? Does the world revolve around you? Do you keep your values and standards high, or do you change because of those around you? Are you the type of friend who you would want to be friends with?

Take some time to reflect on these questions.

As a student in a driver's education class, you're constantly warned about "blind spots"—places where other cars may be hiding that you can't see, even with your rearview and side view mirrors!

It might be a good idea to find someone you trust and ask for help in identifying your personal "blind spots." It could be your parents, a teacher, or a church adviser. Simply ask, "If you ever notice anything that I'm doing that might make it harder for me to make friends, would you please tell me about it?"

It will take some humility, but it can help you recognize some things that will help you. We value the people who will love us enough to be honest with us about the faults we can't see and with kindness and sensitivity let us know how we could work on them to become a better person.

This process of recognizing how your actions and words impact those around you is called "self-awareness." Improving yourself is the first step toward improving your friendships. It starts with you!

CHAPTER 10

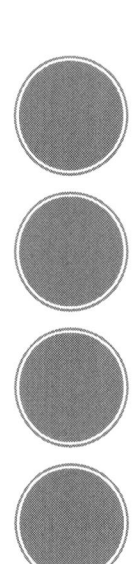

CONCLUSION

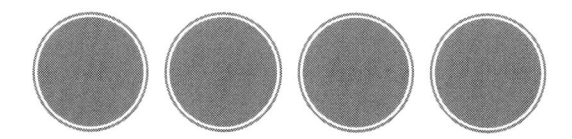

FOCUS ON WHAT YOU CAN CONTROL

Focus on what you can control. The purpose of the Friendship Quadrant isn't to overwhelm you nor make you change all friendships that aren't True Blues (Q1). As stated before, it's a tool and a resource for you to identify the quality of existing friendships, then make some decisions, if need be, on what to do next. That may be distancing yourself from Steer Clears (Q4). It may be looking around at your Steady (Q2) friends and making plans to improve those friendships. It may be recognizing who the Superficials (Q3) are in your life and managing your expectations so you don't get hurt in the future.

Perhaps you now recognize that you have more Steady (Q2) friends and True Blue (Q1) friends than you envisioned. Maybe you realize that you don't have as many quality friends as you thought or would like to have. It may be that you discern you aren't a good friend yourself and you need to change.

There are a variety of things that can be changed. You need to reflect and be boldly honest with yourself as to which quadrant your friendships are in as well as to what kind of friend you are.

You can't control who you'll get along with. You can't change other people's personalities, interests, hobbies, etc. You can't force compatibility. You can't control how your friends will treat you nor where they currently fit in the Friendship Quadrant.

What can you control?

You can control several aspects of the Friendship Quadrant. You can control whom you associate with on a continual basis. You control where you go and what you do. You can control how you treat others. You control what kind of friend you are. You can control you. Most important, you can control your trustworthiness. You can control if you're someone whom all your friends can trust. You can control if you're honest, loyal, kind, reliable, constant, true, sincere, and outward thinking.

If you're lacking in any of these areas, you can change that -- today. You aren't etched in stone. Make a conscious decision to change, and you can. Approach your friends and tell them you want to be better. If apologies are needed on your part, offer them freely. Ask for forgiveness for hurting or offending them in any way. You'll be amazed to see the result of such an approach.

You can change so many people's lives by the type of friend you are. You have the ability to be a force for good. You have the ability to build others up.

Use the Friendship Quadrant as a tool to guide your friendship choices. As you do so, you will enhance your quality of life and experience an increased amount of joy.

> "ALTHOUGH NO ONE CAN GO BACK AND MAKE A BRAND NEW START, ANYONE CAN START FROM NOW AND MAKE A BRAND NEW ENDING."
>
> - CARL BARD -

From our family to yours, thanks for reading the Friendship Quadrant!

Love, The Boyds

Mike, Kassie, Sterling, Savannah, Stefan, Skye & Shepard

LIKE US ON FACEBOOK AND SHARE YOUR STORIES!
WE WOULD LOVE TO HEAR FROM YOU.
SEARCH: "THE FRIENDSHIP QUADRANT"

TO BRING THE FRIENDSHIP QUADRANT
TO YOUR COMMUNITY
VISIT US ONLINE AT:
QUADRANTS4LIFE.COM

Made in the USA
San Bernardino, CA
09 March 2020